Geometry of Design
Studies in Proportion and Composition

Kimberly Elam

Princeton Architectural Press   New York

DESIGN BRIEFS ||||||||||||||| *ESSENTIAL TEXTS ON DESIGN*

ALSO AVAILABLE IN THIS SERIES:
D.I.Y. Design It Yourself, by Ellen Lupton
Elements of Design, by Gail Greet Hannah
Graphic Design Theory, by Helen Armstrong
Grid Systems, by Kimberly Elam
Indie Publishing, by Ellen Lupton
Thinking with Type, by Ellen Lupton
Typographic Systems, by Kimberly Elam
Visual Grammar, by Christian Leborg
The Wayfinding Handbook, by David Gibson

Published by
Princeton Architectural Press
37 East 7th Street
New York, New York 10003

For a free catalog of books, call 1.800.722.6657.
Visit our web site at www.papress.com.

©2001 Princeton Architectural Press
All rights reserved
Printed and bound in China
11 10 09   10 9 8

Project Editor: Jennifer N. Thompson
Designer: Kimberly Elam
Cover Designer: Deb Wood

Special thanks to: Nettie Aljian, Ann Alter, Amanda
Atkins, Janet Behning, Jan Cigliano, Jane Garvie,
Clare Jacobson, Mark Lamster, Nancy Eklund Later,
Brian McDonald, Anne Nitschke, and Lottchen Shivers
of Princeton Architectural Press
—Kevin C. Lippert, publisher

Library of Congress Cataloging-in-Publication Data

Elam, Kimberly, 1951–
  Geometry of design : studies in proportion and composition / Kimberly Elam.
      p. cm. — (Design briefs)
   ISBN 1-56898-249-6 (pbk.)
   1. Proportion (Art) 2. Golden section. 3. Fibonacci
numbers. 4. Composition (Art) 5. Art, Modern—20th
century. I. Title. II. Series.
N7431.5 .E44 2001
   701'.8—dc21
                                    2001000257

Table of Contents

Introduction 5

Proportion in Man and Nature
Cognitive Proportion Preferences 6
Proportion and Nature. 8
Human Body Proportions in Classical Sculpture . 12
Human Body Proportions in Classical Drawing . . 14
Facial Proportions 18

Architectural Proportions
Architectural Proportions. 20
Le Corbusier's Regulating Lines 22

Golden Section
Construction of the Golden Section Rectangle . . 24
Golden Section Proportions 27
Golden Section and the Fibonacci Sequence . . . 29
Golden Section Triangle and Ellipse 30
Golden Section Dynamic Rectangles 32

Root Rectangles
The Root 2 Rectangle Construction 34
DIN System of Paper Proportioning 36
Root 2 Dynamic Rectangles 37
Root 3 Rectangle 38
Root 4 Rectangle 40
Root 5 Rectangle 41
Comparison of Root Rectangles 42

Visual Analysis of Design 43
Folies-Bergère Poster. 44
Job Poster 46
Bauhaus Ausstellung Poster 48
L'Intransigeant Poster 50
East Coast by L.N.E.R. Poster 54
Barcelona Chair 56
Chaise Longue 58
Brno Chair 60
Negerkunst Poster 62
Wagon-Bar Poster 64
Konstruktivisten Poster 66
Der Berufsphotograph Poster 68
Plywood Chair 70
Konkrete Kunst Poster 72
Illinois Institute of Technology Chapel 76
Beethoven Poster. 78
Musica Viva Poster. 82
Pedestal Chair 84
Vormgevers Poster. 86
Fürstenberg Porzellan Poster. 88
Majakovskij Poster 90
Braun Handblender 92
Braun Aromaster Coffee Maker. 94
Il Conico Kettle. 96
Volkswagen Beetle. 98

Postscript 101
Acknowledgments 102
Image & Photo Credits 103
Selected Bibliography. 104
Index. 105

Introduction

Albrecht Dürer
Of the Just Shaping of Letters, 1535
"...sane judgement abhors nothing so much as a picture perpetrated with no technical knowledge, although with plenty of care and diligence. Now the sole reason why painters of this sort are not aware of their own error is that they have not learnt Geometry, without which no one can either be or become an absolute artist; but the blame for this should be laid upon their masters, who themselves are ignorant of this art."

Max Bill
Quoted from Max Bill's writing in 1949, *Typographic Communications Today*, 1989
"I am of the opinion that it is possible to develop an art largely on the basis of mathematical thinking."

Le Corbusier
Towards A New Architecture, 1931
"Geometry is the language of man. ...he has discovered rhythms, rhythms apparent to the eye and clear in their relations with one another. And these rhythms are at the very root of human activities. They resound in man by an organic inevitability, the same fine inevitability which causes the *tracing out of the Golden Section* by children, old men, savages and the learned."

Josef Müller-Brockmann
The Graphic Artist and His Design Problems, 1968
"...the proportions of the formal elements and their intermediate spaces are almost always related to certain numerical progressions logically followed out."

Too often as a design professional and educator I have seen excellent conceptual ideas suffer during the process of realization, in large part because the designer did not understand the visual principles of geometric composition. These principles include an understanding of classic proportioning systems such as the golden section and root rectangles, as well as ratios and proportion, interrelationships of form, and regulating lines. This book seeks to explain visually the principles of geometric composition and offers a wide selection of professional posters, products, and buildings that are visually analyzed by these principles.

The works selected for analysis were selected because they have stood the test of time and in many respects can be considered design classics. The works are arranged in chronological order and have a relationship to the style and technology of the time as well as to the timelessness of classic design. Despite the differences in the era in which the work was created and differences in form, from small two-dimensional graphics to architectural structures, there is a remarkable similarity in the knowledgeable planning and organization through geometry.

The purpose of *Geometry of Design* is not to quantify aesthetics through geometry but rather to reveal visual relationships that have foundations in the essential qualities of life such as proportion and growth patterns as well as mathematics. Its purpose is to lend insight into the design process and give visual coherence to design through visual structure. It is through this insight that the artist or designer may find worth and value for themselves and their own work.

Kimberly Elam
Ringling School of Art and Design
Spring, 2001

5

Cognitive Proportion Preferences

Within the context of the man-made environment and the natural world there is a documented human cognitive preference for golden section proportions throughout recorded history. Some of the earliest evidence of the use of the golden section rectangle, with a proportion of 1:1.618, is documented in the architecture of Stonehenge built in the twentieth to sixteenth centuries, B.C. Further documented evidence is found in the writing, art, and architecture of the ancient Greeks in the fifth century, B.C.. Later, Renaissance artists and architects also studied, documented, and employed golden section proportions in remarkable works of sculpture, painting, and architecture. In addition to man-made works, golden section proportions can also be found in the natural world through human proportions and the growth patterns of many living plants, animals, and insects.

Curious about the golden section a German psychologist, Gustav Fechner, late in the late nineteenth cen-

Table of Rectangle Proportion Preference

Ratio: Width/Length	Most Preferred Rectangle % Fechner	% Lalo	Least Preferred Rectangle % Fechner	% Lalo	
1:1	3.0	11.7	27.8	22.5	square
5:6	0.2	1.0	19.7	16.6	
4:5	2.0	1.3	9.4	9.1	
3:4	2.5	9.5	2.5	9.1	
7:10	7.7	5.6	1.2	2.5	
2:3	20.6	11.0	0.4	0.6	
5:8	35.0	30.3	0.0	0.0	Golden Section Proportion
13:23	20.0	6.3	0.8	0.6	
1:2	7.5	8.0	2.5	12.5	double square
2:5	1.5	15.3	35.7	26.6	
Totals:	100.0	100.0	100.0	100.1	

1:1
square

5:6

4:5

3:4

7:10

tury, investigated the human response to the special aesthetic qualities of the golden section rectangle. Fechner's curiosity was due to the documented evidence of a cross-cultural archetypal aesthetic preference for golden section proportions.

Fechner limited his experiment to the man-made world and began by taking the measurements of thousands of rectangular objects, such as books, boxes, buildings, matchbooks, newspapers, etc. He found that the average rectangle ratio was close to a ratio known as the golden section, 1:1.618, and that the majority of people prefer a rectangle whose proportions are close to the golden section. Fechner's thorough yet casual experiments were repeated later in a more scientific manner by Lalo in 1908 and still later by others, and the results were remarkably similar.

Comparison Graph of Rectangle Preference

Fechner's Graph of Best Rectangle Preference, 1876 ●

Lalo's Graph, 1908 ■

| Ratio | 1:1 square | 5:6 | 4:5 | 3:4 | 7:10 | 2:3 | 5:8 golden section | 13:23 | 1:2 double square | 2:5 |

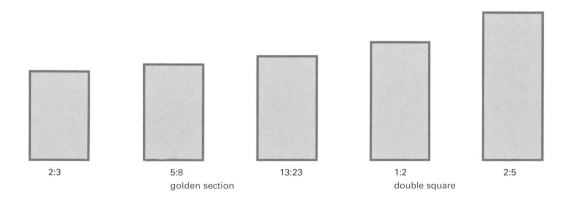

2:3   5:8   13:23   1:2   2:5
          golden section   double square

Proportion and Nature

"The power of the golden section to create harmony arises from its unique capacity to unite different parts of a whole so that each preserves its own identity, and yet blends into the greater pattern of a single whole."
György Doczi, *The Power of Limits, 1994*

Golden section preferences are not limited to human aesthetics but are also a part of the remarkable rela-

tionships between the proportions of patterns of growth in living things such as plants and animals.

The contour spiral shapes of shells reveal a cumulative pattern of growth and these growth patterns have been the subject of many scientific and artistic studies. The growth patterns of shells are logarithmic spirals of golden section proportions, and what is known as the theory of a perfect growth pattern. Theodore Andreas

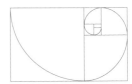

Golden Section Spiral Construction diagram of the golden section rectangle and resulting spiral.

Chambered Nautilus
Cross section of the Nautilus' spiral growth pattern.

8

Atlantic Sundial Shell
Spiral growth pattern.

Moon Snail Shell
Spiral growth pattern.

Cook in his book *The Curves of Life* describes these growth patterns as "the essential processes of life...." In each growth phase characterized by a spiral, the new spiral is very close to the proportion of a golden section square larger than the previous one. The growth patterns of the nautilus and other shells are never exact golden section proportions. Rather, there is an attempt in biological growth pattern proportion to approach but never reach exact golden spiral proportions.

The pentagon and pentagram star also share golden section proportions and can be found in many living things such as the sand dollar. The interior subdivisions of a pentagon create a star pentagram, and the ratio of any two lines within a star pentagram is the golden section proportion of 1:1.618.

Comparison of Tibia Shell Spiral Growth Pattern and Golden Section Proportion

Pentagon Pattern
The pentagon and star pentagram have golden section proportions, as the ratios of the sides of the triangles in a star pentagram is 1:1.618. The same pentagon/pentagram relationships can be found in the sand dollar and in snowflakes.

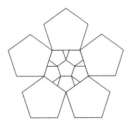
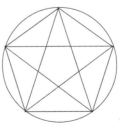

The spiral growth patterns of the pine cone and the sunflower share similar growth patterns. The seeds of each grow along two intersecting spirals which move in opposite directions, and each seed belongs to both sets of intersecting spirals. Upon examining the pine cone seed spirals, 8 of the spirals move in a clockwise direction and 13 in a counterclockwise direction, closely approximating golden section proportions. In the case of the sunflower spirals there are 21 clockwise spirals and 34 counter clockwise spirals, which again approximate golden section proportions.

The numbers 8 and 13 as found in the pine cone spiral and 21 and 34 as found in the sunflower spiral are very familiar to mathematicians. They are adjacent pairs in the mathematical sequence called the Fibonacci sequence. Each number in the sequence is determined by adding together the previous two: 0, 1, 1, 2, 3, 5, 8, 13, 21, 34,

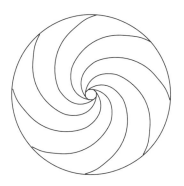 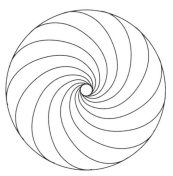 

Spiral Growth Patterns of Pine Cones

Each seed in the pine cone belongs to both sets of spirals. 8 of the spirals move clockwise and 13 of the spirals move counterclockwise. The proportion of 8:13 is 1:1.625 which is very close to the golden section proportion of 1:1.618

Spiral Growth Patterns of Sunflowers

Similar to the pine cone each seed in the sunflower belongs to both sets of spirals. 21 spirals move clockwise, and 34 spirals move counterclockwise. The proportion of 21:34 is 1:1.619 which is very close to the golden section proportion of 1:1.618

10

55.... The ratio of adjacent numbers in the sequence progressively approaches golden section proportions of 1:1.618.

Many fish also share relationships with the golden section. Three golden section construction diagrams placed on the body of the rainbow trout show the relationships of the eye and the tail fin in the reciprocal golden rectangles and square. Further, the individual fins also have a golden sec-

tion proportions. The blue angle tropical fish fits perfectly into a golden section rectangle and the mouth and gills are on the reciprocal golden section point of the body's height.

Perhaps a part of our human fascination with the natural environment and living things such as shells, flowers, and fish is due to our subconscious preference for golden section proportions, shapes, and patterns.

reciprocal golden section rectangle

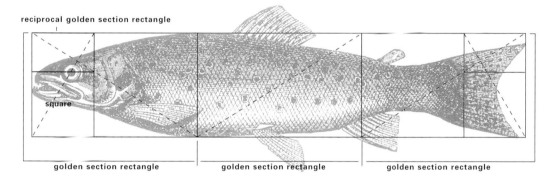

square

golden section rectangle   golden section rectangle   golden section rectangle

Golden Section Analysis of a Trout
The body of the trout is enclosed by three golden section rectangles. The eye is at the level of the reciprocal golden rectangle and the tail fin is defined by a reciprocal golden rectangle.

Golden Section Analysis of a Blue Angle Fish
The entire body of the fish fits into a golden section rectangle. The mouth and gill position is at the reciprocal golden section rectangle.

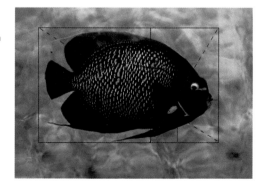

Human Body Proportions in Classical Sculpture

Just as many plants and animals share golden section proportions, humans do as well. Perhaps another reason for the cognitive preference for golden section proportions is that the human face and body share the similar mathematical proportional relationships found in all living things.

Some of the earliest surviving written investigations into human proportion and architecture are in the writings of the ancient Roman scholar and architect

Marcus Vitruvius Pollio, who is widely referred to as Vitruvius. Vitruvius advised that the architecture of temples should be based on the likeness of the perfectly proportioned human body where a harmony exists among all parts. Vitruvius described this proportion and explained that the height of a well proportioned man is equal to the length of his outstretched arms. The body height and length of the outstretched arms create a square that enclose the human body, while the hands and feet touch a circle

Golden Section Proportions of Greek Sculpture
Doryphoros, the Spear Bearer (left). *Statue of Zeus from Cape Artemision* (right). Each golden section rectangle is represented by a rectangle with a dashed diagonal line. Multiple golden section rectangles share the dashed diagonal. The proportions of the two figures are almost identical.

with the navel as the center. Within this system the human form is divided in half at the groin, and by the golden section at the navel. The statues of the *Spear Bearer* and *Zeus* are both from the fifth century B.C. Although created by different sculptors, the proportions of the *Spear Bearer* and *Zeus* are both clearly based on the canon of Vitruvius and the analysis of the proportions used is almost identical.

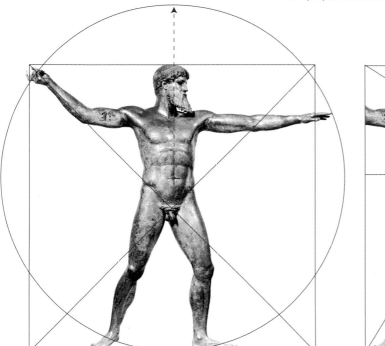

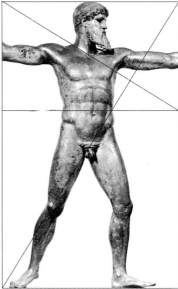

***Zeus* Analyzed According to the Vitruvius' Canon**
A square encloses the body while the hands and feet touch a circle with the navel as center. The figure is divided in half at the groin, and (far right) by the golden section at the navel.

Human Body Proportions in Classical Drawing

The Vitruvius canon, was also used by Renaissance artists Leonardo da Vinci and Albrecht Dürer in the late fifteenth and early sixteenth centuries. Both da Vinci and Dürer were students and scholars of proportioning systems of the human form. Dürer experimented with a number of proportioning systems that were illustrated in his books, *Four Books on Human Proportion,* 1528. da Vinci illustrated the mathematician Luca Pacioli's book, *Divina Proportione*, 1509.

Individually, both da Vinci's and Dürer's drawings clearly conform to the proportioning system of Vitruvius. Further, an overlay comparison of da Vinci's and Dürer's proportion drawings reveals that the body proportions in both drawings share the proportions of Vitruvius and that the two are almost identical. The only significant differences are in the facial proportions.

Man Inscribed in a Circle, **Albrecht Dürer, After 1521**

Human Figure in a Circle, Illustrating Proportions, **Leonardo da Vinci, 1485–1490**

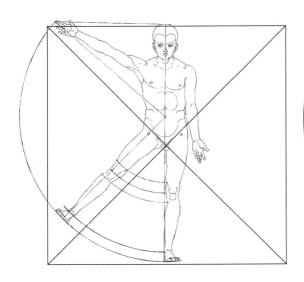

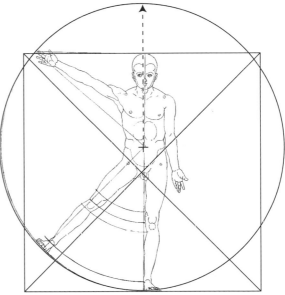

**The Canon of Vitruvius applied to Dürer's draw-
ing of *Man Inscribed in a Circle***
A square encloses the body while the hands and feet
touch a circle with the navel as center. The figure is
divided in half at the groin, and by the golden section
at the navel.

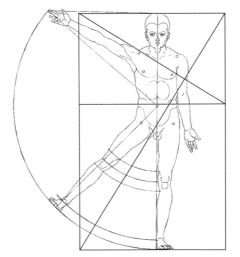

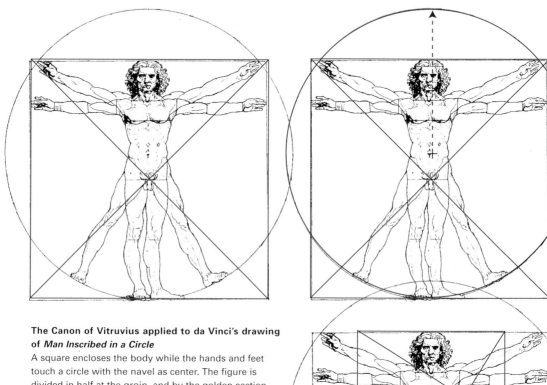

16

The Canon of Vitruvius applied to da Vinci's drawing of *Man Inscribed in a Circle*

A square encloses the body while the hands and feet touch a circle with the navel as center. The figure is divided in half at the groin, and by the golden section at the navel.

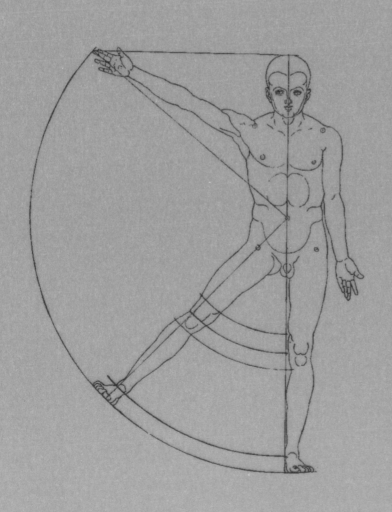

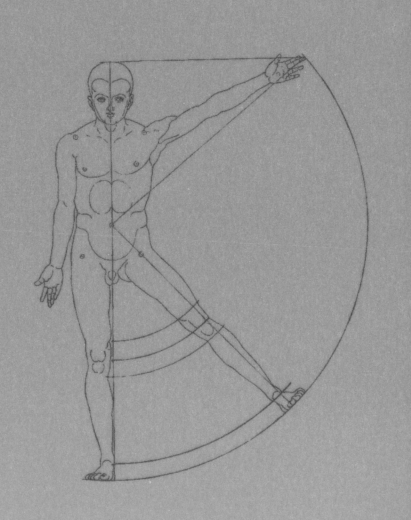

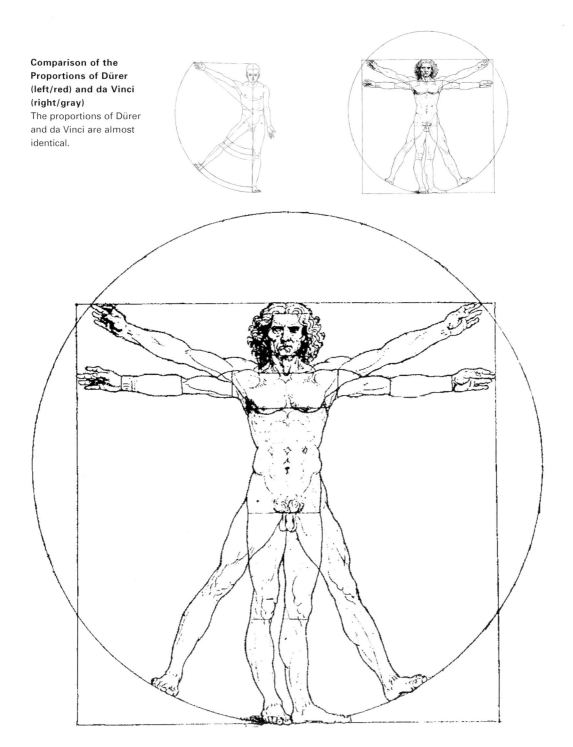

**Comparison of the
Proportions of Dürer
(left/red) and da Vinci
(right/gray)**
The proportions of Dürer
and da Vinci are almost
identical.

17

Facial Proportions

The canon of Vitruvius includes human facial proportions as well as body proportions. The placement of the facial features yields the classic proportions used in Greek and Roman sculpture.

While both Leonardo da Vinci and Albrecht Dürer employed Vitruvius' canon of body proportions, dramatic differences exist in the facial proportions. da Vinci's system for the face mirrors that of Vitruvius

and faint construction lines can be seen in his original drawing of human proportions.

Dürer, however, uses distinctly different facial proportions. Dürer's facial proportions in his *Man Inscribed in a Circle* drawing are characterized by low set facial features and a high forehead, which is possibly an aesthetic preference of the fashion of the time. The face is divided in half by a line at the top of

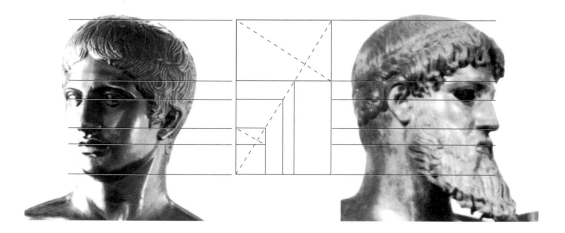

Comparison of Facial Proportions and the Golden Section
Detail of the head of *Doryphoros, the Spear Bearer* (left). Detail of the Head of the *Statue of Zeus from Cape Artemision* (right). Facial proportion analysis is according to Vitruvius' canon, and the proportions are almost

identical. The diagram shows a single golden section rectangle as the guide for the length and width of the head. This golden rectangle is further subdivided by smaller golden section rectangles to determine the placement of the features.

Dürer's Facial Proportion Studies
Four samples from *Four Constructed Heads, Studies in Physiognomy,* About 1526–27.

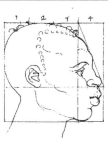

the eye brows, with the features of eyes, nose, and mouth below this line, and shortened neck. The same facial proportions are repeatedly used throughout many drawings in the book *Four Books on Human Proportion*, 1528. Dürer also experiments with facial proportion in the drawing, *Four Constructed Heads*, in which he introduces oblique lines into the construction grid to produce variations.

Humans like other living things very rarely attain perfect golden section facial or body proportions, except through the artists vision in drawing, painting, and sculpture. The use of golden section proportions by artists, particularly the ancient Greeks, was an attempt to idealize and systemize the representation of the human body

Comparison of Facial Proportions of drawings by da Vinci and Dürer
Detail of the head of da Vinci's *Human Figure in a Circle* (left), and a detail of the head of Dürer's drawing of *Man Inscribed in a Circle* (right). da Vinci's facial proportions match the canon of Vitruvius, whereas Dürer's facial proportions are distinctly different.

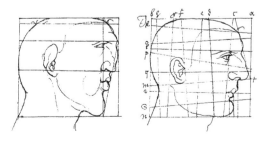

Architectural Proportions

In addition to documenting human body proportions Vitruvius was also an architect and documented harmonious architectural proportions. He advocated that the architecture of temples should be based on the perfectly proportioned human body where there exists a harmony between all parts. He is credited with introducing the concept of the module, in the same way as the human proportions were expressed in a module representing the length of the head or feet. This concept became an important idea throughout the history of architecture.

The *Parthenon* in Athens is an example of the Greek system of proportioning. In a simple analysis the façade of the parthenon is embraced by a subdivided golden rectangle. A reciprocal rectangle forms the height of the architrave, frieze, and pediment. The square of the main rectangle gives the height of the pediment, and the smallest rectangle in the diagram yields the placement of the frieze and architrave.

Centuries later the "divine proportion," or golden section, was consciously employed in the architecture of

Drawing of the *Parthenon*, Athens, ca. 447–432 B.C., and the Architectural Relationship to the Golden Section
Analysis of golden section proportions according to the golden section construction diagram.

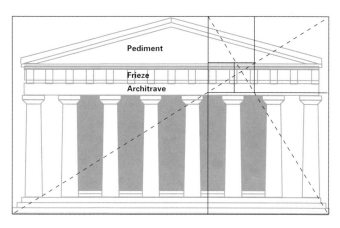

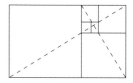

Golden Section Harmonic Analysis
Analysis of golden section proportions according to a diagram of a harmonic analysis of the golden section.

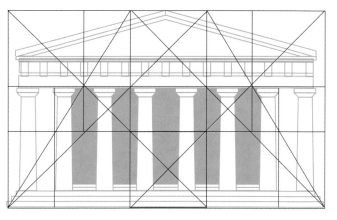

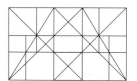

Gothic cathedrals. In *Towards A New Architecture*, Le Corbusier cites the role of the square and the circle in the proportions of the façade of the Cathedral of Notre Dame, Paris. The rectangle around the cathedral façade is in golden section proportion. The square of this golden section rectangle encloses the major portion of the façade, and the reciprocal golden section rectangle encloses the two towers. The regulating lines are the diagonals that meet just above the clerestory window, crossing the corners of the major variations in the surface of the cathedral. The center front doorway is also in golden section proportion as shown by the construction diagram. The proportion of the clerestory window is one-fourth the diameter of the circle inscribed in the square.

Notre Dame Cathedral, Paris, 1163 –1235

Analysis of proportions and regulating lines according to the golden section rectangle. The entire façade is in golden rectangle proportion. The lower portion of the façade is enclosed by the square of the golden rectangle and the towers are enclosed by the reciprocal golden section rectangle. Further, the lower portion of the façade can be divided into six units, each another golden rectangle.

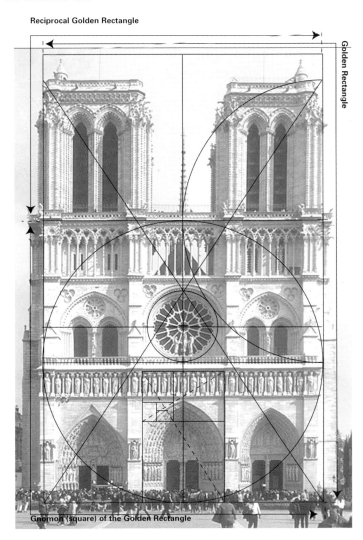

Reciprocal Golden Rectangle

Golden Rectangle

Gnomon (square) of the Golden Rectangle

21

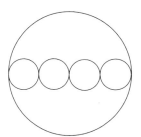

Proportion Comparison

The clerestory window is in proportion of 1:4 to the major circle of the façade.

Le Corbusier's Regulating Lines

Le Corbusier
Towards a New Architecture, 1931
"An inevitable element of Architecture. The necessity for order. The regulating line is a guarantee against willfulness. It brings satisfaction to the understanding. The regulating line is a means to an end; it is not a recipe. Its choice and the modalities of expression given to it are an integral part of architectural creation"

Corbusier's interest in the application of the geometry of structure and mathematics is recorded in his book *Towards a New Architecture*. Here he discusses the need for regulating lines as a means to create order and beauty in architecture and answers the criticism, "With your regulating lines you kill imagination, you make a god of a recipe." He responds, "But the past has left us proofs, iconographical documents, eteles, slabs, incised stones, parchments, manuscripts, printed matter.... Even the earliest and

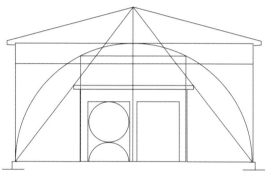 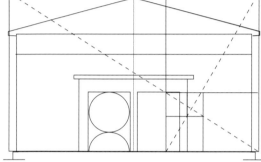

Redrawn from the Marble Slab Found in 1882, *Facade of the Arsenal of the Piraes.* **Le Corbusier,** *Towards a New Architecture,* **1931**
Corbusier cites the regulated lines of simple divisions that determine the proportion of the height to the width, and guide the placement of the doors and their proportion to the facade. The facade fits into a golden section rectangle and the placement and height of the doorway corresponds to that proportion.

most primitive architect developed the use of a regulating unit of measure such as a hand, or foot, or forearm in order to systemize and bring order to the task. At the same time the proportions of the structure corresponded to human scale."

Corbusier discusses the regulating line as "...one of the decisive moments of inspiration, it is one of the vital operations of architecture." Later, in 1942, Le Corbusier published *The Modulor: A Harmonious*

Measure to the Human Scale Universally Applicable to Architecture and Mechanics. The Modulor chronicled his proportioning system on the mathematics of the golden section and the proportion of the human body.

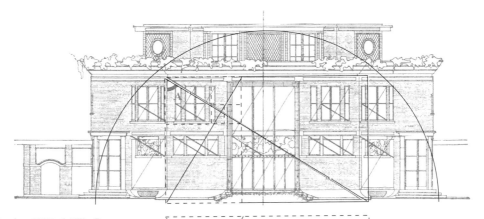

Le Corbusier, 1916. *A Villa*, From *Towards a New Architecture*, 1931 (above) This drawing by Le Corbusier diagrams the series of regulating lines that were used in the building design. Red lines placed on top of the drawing show the golden section rectangle and construction diagonals.

Golden Section Construction (right) The relationship of Corbusier's regulating lines to the two construction diagrams of the golden section rectangle.

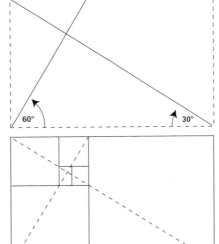

Construction of the Golden Section Rectangle

The golden section rectangle is a ratio of the Divine Proportion. The Divine Proportion is derived from the division of a line segment into two segments such that the ratio of the whole segment, AB, to the longer part, AC, is the same as the ratio of the longer part, AC, to the shorter part, CB. This gives a ratio of approximately 1.61803 to 1, which can also be expressed $\frac{1+\sqrt{5}}{2}$.

The Divine Proportion:

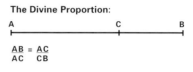

$$\frac{AB}{AC} = \frac{AC}{CB}$$

Golden Section, Square Construction Method

1. Begin with a square.

2. Draw a diagonal from the midpoint A of one of the sides to an opposite corner B. This diagonal becomes the radius of an arc that extends beyond the square to C. The smaller rectangle and the square become a golden section rectangle.

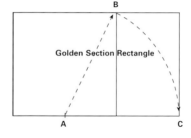

3. The golden section rectangle can be subdivided. When subdivided the rectangle produces a smaller proportional golden section rectangle which is the reciprocal, and a square area remains after subdivision. This square area can also be called a gnomon.

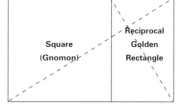

4. The process of subdivision can endlessly continue, again and again, producing smaller proportional rectangles and squares.

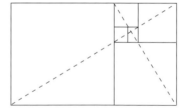

The golden section rectangle is unique in that when subdivided its reciprocal is a smaller proportional rectangle and the area remaining after subdivision is a square. Because of the special property of subdividing into a reciprocal rectangle and a square, the golden section rectangle is known as the whirling square rectangle. The proportionally decreasing squares can produce a spiral by using a radius the length of the sides of the square.

Golden Section Spiral Construction
By using the golden section subdivision diagram a golden section spiral can be constructed. Use the length of the sides of the squares of the subdivisions as a radius of a circle. Strike and connect arcs for each square in the diagram.

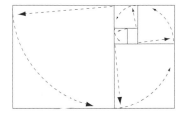

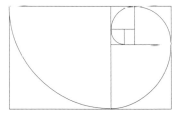

Proportional Squares
The squares from the golden section subdivision diagram are in golden section proportion to each other.

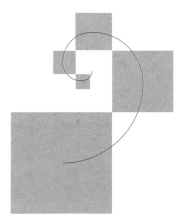

Golden Section Rectangle, Triangle Construction Method

1. Begin with a right triangle whose sides are in 1:2 proportion. Draw an arc from D using DA as a radius, that crosses the hypotenuse.

2. Draw another arc along the hypotenuse from C using CE as a radius to intersect the base line.

3. From point B where the arc intersects the base line draw a vertical that touches the hypotenuse.

4. This method produces golden section proportions by defining the length of the sides of the rectangle, AB and BC. The subdivision of the triangle yields sides of a rectangle in golden ratio proportion, since the ratio of AB to BC is a golden section ratio of 1:1.618.

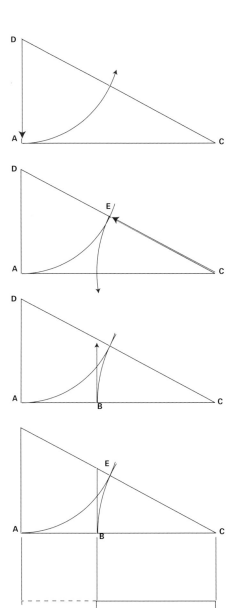

Golden Section Proportions

The divisions and proportion of the triangle method of the golden section construction produce the sides of a golden section rectangle, and in addition, the method can produce a series of circles or squares that are in golden section proportion to each other as in the examples below.

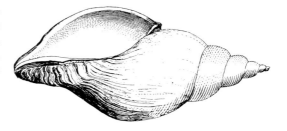

Diameter AB = BC + CD
Diameter BC = CD + DE
Diameter CD = DE + EF
etc.

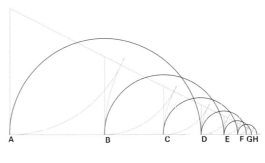

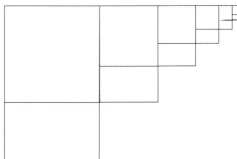

Golden Rectangle +	Square =	Golden Rectangle
A	+ B	= AB
AB	+ C	= ABC
ABC	+ D	= ABCD
ABCD	+ E	= ABCDE
ABCDE	+ F	= ABCDEF
ABCDEF	+ G	= ABCDEFG

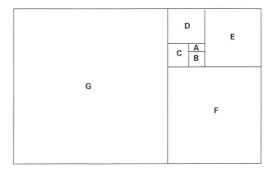

Golden Section Proportions in Circles and Squares

The triangle construction method of the golden section will also yield a series of circles or squares in golden section proportion.

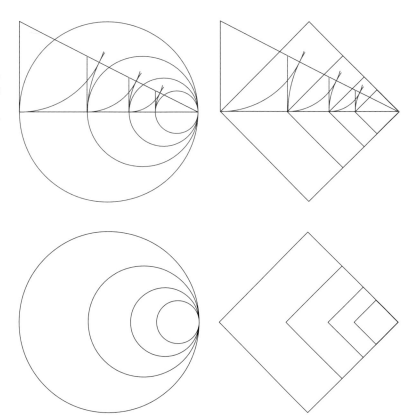

Golden Section and the Fibonacci Sequence

The special proportioning properties of the golden section have a close relationship to a sequence of numbers called the Fibonacci sequence, named for Leonardo of Pisa who introduced it to Europe about eight hundred years ago along with the decimal system. This sequence of numbers, 1, 1, 2, 3, 5, 8, 13, 21, 34... is calculated by adding the two previous numbers to produce the third. For example, 1+1=2, 1+2=3, 2+3=5 etc. The proportioning pattern of this system is very close to the proportioning system of the golden section. The early numbers in the sequence begin to approach the golden section, and any number beyond the fifteenth number in the sequence that is divided by the following number approximates 0.618, and any number divided by the previous number approximates 1.618.

Fibonacci Number Sequence

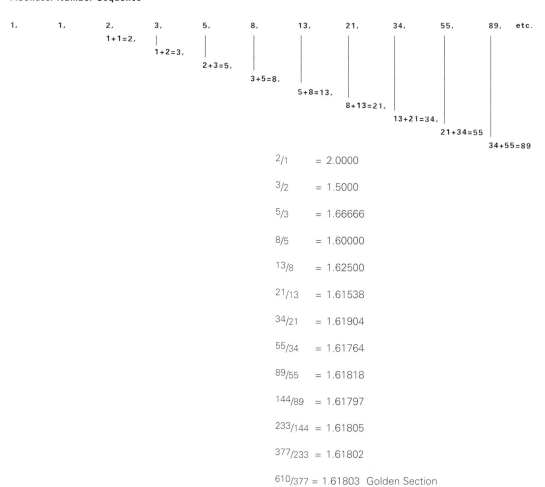

1,	1,	2,	3,	5,	8,	13,	21,	34,	55,	89,	etc.
		1+1=2,	1+2=3,	2+3=5,	3+5=8,	5+8=13,	8+13=21,	13+21=34,	21+34=55	34+55=89	

$2/1$ = 2.0000

$3/2$ = 1.5000

$5/3$ = 1.66666

$8/5$ = 1.60000

$13/8$ = 1.62500

$21/13$ = 1.61538

$34/21$ = 1.61904

$55/34$ = 1.61764

$89/55$ = 1.61818

$144/89$ = 1.61797

$233/144$ = 1.61805

$377/233$ = 1.61802

$610/377$ = 1.61803 Golden Section

29

Golden Section Triangle and Ellipse

The golden section triangle is an isosceles triangle, having two equal sides, and is also known as the "sublime" triangle, as it has similar aesthetic properties to the golden section rectangle; it is the preferred triangle of a majority of people. It is readily constructed from a pentagon and will have an angle of 36° at the vertex and angles of 72° at the base. This construction can be further divided into another golden triangle by connecting the base angle of the larger triangle to a vertex of the pentagon at the opposite side. A continued connection

of the vertices with the diagonals will result in a star pentagram. The decagon, a ten-sided polygon, will also yield a series of golden triangles by connecting the center point to any two adjacent vertices.

The golden ellipse also has been shown to have similar aesthetic qualities to the golden section rectangle and the golden section triangle. Like the rectangle, it has the same proportion of the major to minor axis of 1:1.618.

Golden Section Triangle Constructed From a Pentagon
Begin with a pentagon. Connect the angles at the base of the pentagon to the vertex of the pentagon. This will result in a golden section triangle with base angles of 72° and a vertex of 36°.

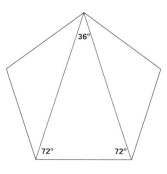

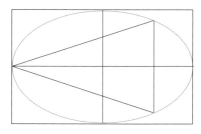

Golden Section Ellipse Inscribed Inside a Golden Section Rectangle

Secondary Golden Section Triangle Constructed From a Pentagon
The pentagon construction will also yield secondary golden section triangles. Connect a base angle to a vertex at the opposite side.

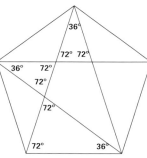

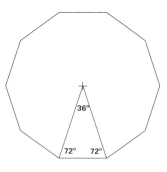

Golden Section Triangle Inscribed in a Golden Section Ellipse, Inscribed in a Golden Section Rectangle

Golden Section Triangle Constructed From a Decagon
Begin with a decagon, a ten sided polygon. Connect any two adjacent vertices to the center to yield a golden section rectangle.

Golden Section Proportions of the Star Pentagram

The five-pointed star created by the diagonals of a regular pentagon is a star pentagram, whose central part is another pentagon, etc. The progression of smaller pentagons and pentagrams is known as Pythagoras's lute, because of the relationship to the golden section.

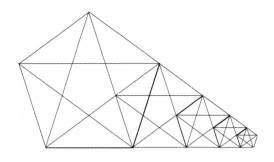

Golden Section Spiral Created With Golden Section Triangles

A golden section triangle can be subdivided into a series of smaller golden section triangles by striking a new angle of 36° from the base angle. The spiral is created by using the length of the sides of the triangles of the subdivisions as a radius of a circle.

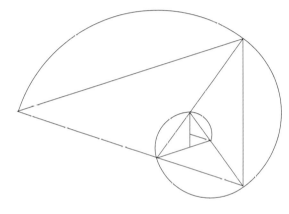

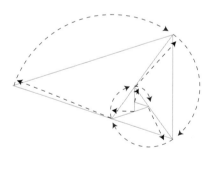

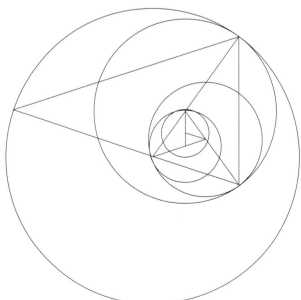

Golden Section Dynamic Rectangles

All rectangles can be divided into two categories: static rectangles with ratios of rational fractions such as 1/2, 2/3, 3/3, 3/4, etc., and dynamic rectangles with ratios of irrational fractions such as √2, √3, √5, φ (golden section), etc. Static rectangles do not produce a series of visually pleasing ratios of surfaces when subdivided. The subdivisions are anticipated and regular without much variation. However, dynamic rectangles produce an endless amount of visually pleas-

ing harmonic subdivisions and surface ratios when subdivided, because their ratios consist of irrational numbers.

The process of subdividing a dynamic rectangle into a series of harmonic subdivisions is very simple. Diagonals are struck from opposite corners and then a network of parallel and perpendicular lines are constructed to the sides and diagonals.

Golden Section Dynamic Rectangles
These diagrams from *The Geometry of Art and Life,* illustrate a range of harmonic subdivisions of golden section rectangles. The small red line rectangles (left) show the golden section rectangle construction. The gray and red rectangles (middle) show the red golden section rectangle construction with the harmonic subdivisions in gray line. The black line rectangles (right) show only the harmonic subdivisions.

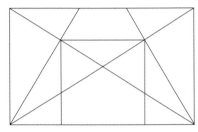
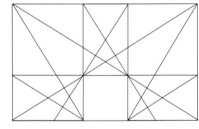

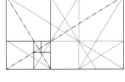
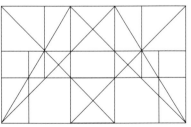
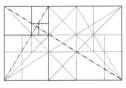

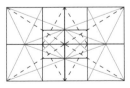
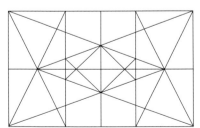

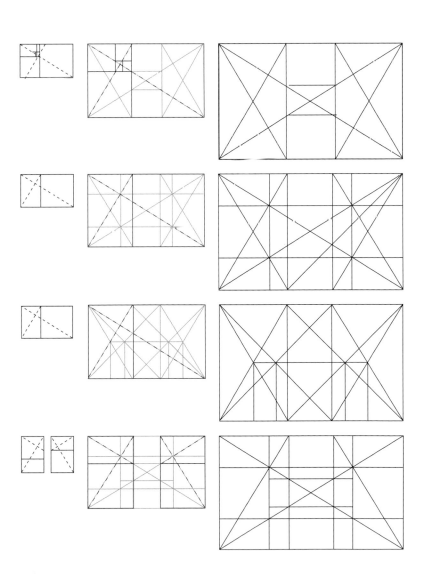

The Root 2 Rectangle Construction

Root 2 rectangles possess the special property of being endlessly subdivided into proportionally smaller rectangles. This means that when a root 2 rectangle is divided in half, the result is two smaller root 2 rectangles; when divided into fourths, the result is four smaller root 2 rectangles, etc.

It should also be noted that the proportion of the root 2 rectangle approximates, rather closely, golden section proportions. Root 2 proportions are 1:1.41 and golden section proportions are 1:1.618.

**Root 2 Rectangle Construction,
Square Method**
1. Begin with a square.

2. Draw a diagonal within the square. Use the diagonal as an arc that touches the square base line. Enclose a rectangle around the new figure. This is a root 2 rectangle.

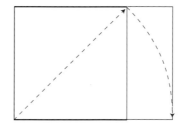

Root 2 Subdivision
1. The root 2 rectangle can be subdivided into smaller root 2 rectangles. Subdivide the rectangle in half via a diagonal creating two smaller rectangles. Again subdivide the halves into smaller root 2 rectangles.

2. This process can be repeated endlessly to create an infinite series of root 2 rectangles.

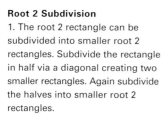

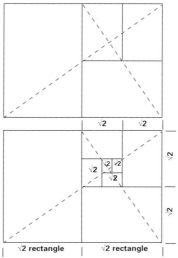

Root 2 Rectangle Construction, Circle Method
1. Another method of constructing a root 2 rectangle is by beginning with a circle. Inscribe a square in the circle.

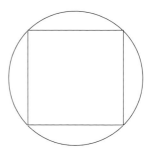

2. Extend the two opposite sides of the square so that they touch the circle. The resulting rectangle is a root 2 rectangle.

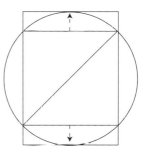

Root 2 Diminishing Spiral
A root 2 diminishing spiral can be created by striking and connecting diagonals on reciprocal root 2 rectangles.

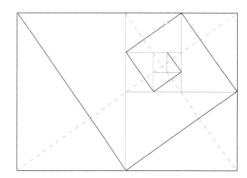

Root 2 Proportional Relationships
Subdividing a root 2 rectangle continuously produces smaller proportional root 2 rectangles.

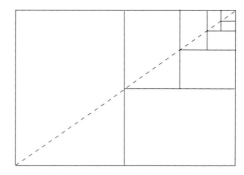

DIN System of Paper Proportioning

Root 2 rectangles possess the special property of being endlessly subdivided by proportionally smaller rectangles. It is for this reason that the root 2 rectangle is the basis for the European DIN (Deutsche Industrie Normen), a system of paper sizes. Therefore, it is also the same proportion of many of the European posters examined in this book. Folding the sheet once produces the half sheet or folio. The sheet folded four times results in 4 leaves or 8 printed pages, etc.. This system is not only efficient but also optimizes the use of paper through a system that has no waste. European cities with a rich poster tradition have standardized display areas of street posters in this proportion. Not only does the root 2 rectangle have the functional property of eliminating waste but also closely follows the aesthetic properties of the golden section.

Root 2 Dynamic Rectangles

Similar to the golden section rectangle, root 2 rectangles are known as dynamic rectangles because, like golden section rectangles, they produce a variety of harmonic subdivisions and combinations that are always related to the proportions of the original rectangle.

The process of harmonic subdivision consists of drawing diagonals and then drawing a network of par-

allel and perpendicular lines to the sides and diagonals. The root 2 rectangle will always subdivide into an equal number of reciprocals.

Harmonic Subdivisions of Root 2 Rectangles
(left) Division of a root 2 rectangle into sixteen smaller root 2 rectangles.
(right) Division of a root 2 rectangle into four columns and adjacent angles.

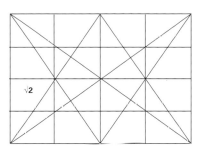
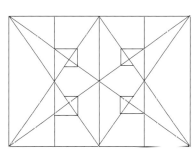

(left) Division of a root 2 rectangle into nine smaller root 2 rectangles.
(right) Division of a Root 2 Rectangle into three smaller root 2 rectangles and three squares.

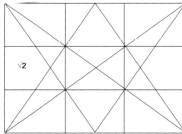
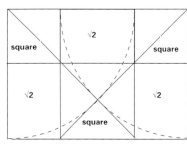

(left) Division of a root 2 rectangle into five root 2 rectangles and two squares.
(right) Division of two root 2 rectangles.

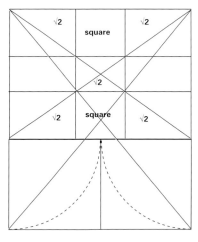
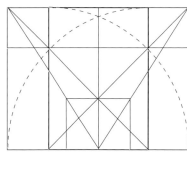

Root 3 Rectangle

Just as the root 2 rectangle can be divided into other similar rectangles, so too can the root 3, root 4, and root 5 rectangles. These rectangles can be subdivided both horizontally and vertically. The root 3 rectangle can be subdivided into three root 3 vertical rectangles; these vertical rectangles can be subdivided into three root 3 horizontal rectangles, etc.

The root 3 rectangle has the property of enabling the construction of a regular hexagonal prism. This hexa-

gon can be found in the shape of snow crystals, honeycombs, and in many other facets of the natural world.

Root 3 Construction
1. Begin with a root 2 rectangle.

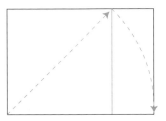

2. Draw a diagonal within the root 2 rectangle. Use the diagonal as an arc that touches the square base line. Enclose a rectangle around the new figure. This is a root 3 rectangle.

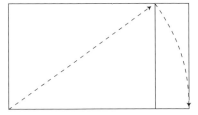

Root 3 Subdivision
The root 3 rectangle can be subdivided into smaller root 3 rectangles. Subdivide the rectangle in thirds to create three smaller rectangles. Again subdivide the thirds into smaller root 3 rectangles. This process can be repeated endlessly to create an infinite series of root 3 rectangles.

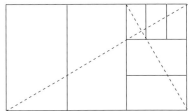

Hexagon Construction

A hexagon can be constructed from a root 3 rectangle. This is done by rotating the rectangle from a center axis so that the corners meet.

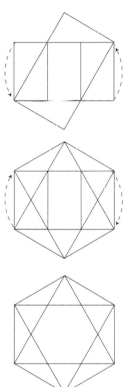

Root 4 Construction

1. Begin with a root 3 rectangle.

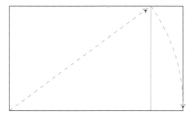

2. Draw a diagonal within the root 3 rectangle. Use the diagonal as an arc that touches the square base line. Enclose a rectangle around the new figure. This is a root 4 rectangle.

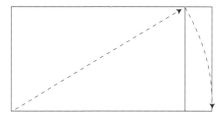

Root 4 Subdivision

The root 4 rectangle can be subdivided into smaller root 4 rectangles. Subdivide the rectangle into fourths, creating four smaller rectangles. Again subdivide the fourths into smaller root 4 rectangles. This process can be repeated endlessly to create an infinite series of root 4 rectangles.

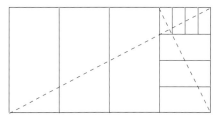

Root 5 Rectangle

Root 5 Construction
1. Begin with a root 4 rectangle.

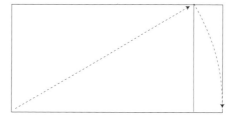

2. Draw a diagonal within the root 4 rectangle. Use the diagonal as an arc that touches the square base line. Enclose a rectangle around the new figure. This is a root 5 rectangle.

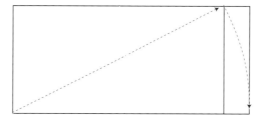

Root 5 Subdivision
The root 5 rectangle can be subdivided into smaller root 5 rectangles. Subdivide the rectangle in fifths to create five smaller rectangles. Again subdivide the fifths into smaller root 5 rectangles. This process can be repeated endlessly to create an infinite series of root 5 rectangles.

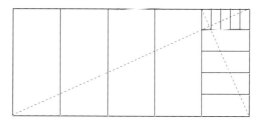

Root 5, Square Construction Method
Another method for construction of a root 5 rectangle begins with a square. An arc is struck from the center of the bottom edge of a square. Then the square is extended to include the arcs on both sides.

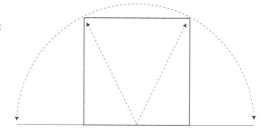

41

The small rectangles on either side of the square are golden rectangles, and one of the small rectangles and the center square form another golden rectangle. Both golden rectangles and the square are form a root 5 rectangle.

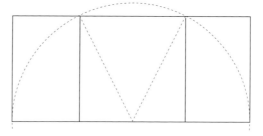

Comparison of Root Rectangles

√2 √3 √4 √5

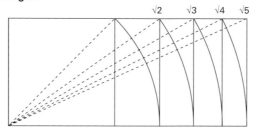 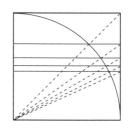

√2

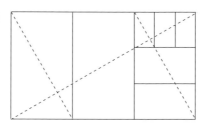

√3

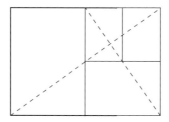

42

√4

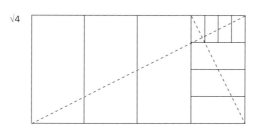

√5

Visual Analysis of Design

There is no better way to begin to view the analysis of graphic design, illustration, architecture, and industrial design than with an introduction by Le Corbusier.

In *The Modulor*, Le Corbusier writes of his revelation as a young man in Paris: "One day, under the oil lamp in his little room in Paris, some picture postcards were spread out on his table. His eye lingered on a picture of Michelangelo's Capitol in Rome. He turned over another card, face downward, and intuitively projected one of its angles (a right angle) on to the façade of the Capitol. Suddenly he was struck afresh by a familiar truth: the right angle governs the composition; the *lieux* (*lieu de l'angle droit*: place of the right angle) command(s) the entire composition. This was to him a revelation, a certitude. The same test worked with a painting by Cézanne. But he mistrusted his own verdict, saying to himself that the composition of works of art is governed by rules; these rules may be conscious methods, pointed and subtle, or they may be commonplace rules, tritely applied. They may also be *implied* by the creative instinct of the artist, a manifestation of an intuitive harmony, as was almost certainly the case with Cézanne: Michelangelo being of a different nature, with a tendency to follow preconceived and deliberate, conscious designs.

A book brought him certainty: some pages in Auguste Choisy's book on the *History of Architecture* devoted to the tracé regulateur (regulating lines). So there were such things as regulating lines to govern composition?

In 1918 he began to paint in earnest. The first two pictures were composed haphazardly. The third, in 1919, was an attempt to cover the canvas in an ordered manner. The result was almost good. Then came the fourth painting, reproducing the third in an improved form, with a categorical design to hold it together, enclose it, give it a structure. Then came a series of pictures painted in 1920 (exhibited at the Galerie Druet, 1921); all these are firmly founded on geometry. Two mathematical expedients were used in these paintings: the place of the right angle and the golden mean."

Corbusier's revelation is one that is of value for all artists, designers, and architects. The understanding of the underlying organizational principles of geometry brings to a creative work a sense of compositional cohesiveness, whereby each element of the work has a visual sense of belonging. By revealing some of the geometry, systems, and proportions it is possible to understand better the intent and reasoning of a number of designers and architects. It gives insight into the process of realization and a rational explanation for many decisions, whether the use of organizational geometry is intuitive or deliberate, rigidly applied or casually considered.

Folies-Bergère Poster, Jules Chéret, 1877

Folies-Bergère by Jules Chéret is an engaging and dynamic work that captures the movement of a group of dancers. At first glance the composition appears spontaneous and without geometric organization but closer examination reveals a very carefully developed visual structure. The positions of the dancers limbs closely correspond to a pentagon embraced by a circle.

The interior subdivisions of the pentagon create star pentagrams which in turn create a smaller proportional pentagon. The ratio of the sides of the triangles within a star pentagram is 1: 1.618, the golden section ratio. The exact center of the poster is a pivot point on the female dancer's hip, and the legs of the male dancers create an inverted triangle, the top point of the pentagram star, that embraces the female dancer. Each limb and shoulder is carefully positioned according to the geometry of the structure.

The Star Pentagram

The subdivisions of the pentagon create an interior star whose center is a pentagram. The golden section is present in that the triangles have two equal sides, B or C, that relate to the third side, A, as 1:1.618, the golden section ratio.

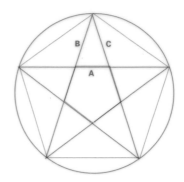

Analysis

The three figures are embraced first by a circle, then by a pentagon, next by a star pentagram and finally by a pentagon, with the center as a pivot point from the female dancer's hip. Even the small elfin figure at the bottom plays into this structure as the head meets the circle and pentagon.

(below) The triangle created by the dancers legs is a golden section triangle.

Job Poster, Jules Chéret, 1889

Chéret was a master lithographer and is credited with elevating the chromolithography printing process to an art form. His knowledge of chromolithography printing grew from an apprenticeship begun at age 13. The only formal education he received in art and design was a course at the École Nationale de Dessin, National School of Design. It is perhaps in this course that he was introduced to geometry and the principles of composition. Although his formal education was limited, throughout his career he made the major art museums of Europe his personal schools and carefully studied the works of the masters.

Many of Chéret's posters were instant successes because of the beautiful play in color and the delightful illustrated figures. He understood the chromolithographic printing process and used it to his advantage. He also understood the principles of composition and used them to unify this and many other works.

The Star Pentagram and Format Proportion

Expanding the star pentagram inscribed in a circle reveals that the poster format proportions are based on this system known as the "pentagon page." The base of the poster conforms to the bottom side of the pentagram and is extended so that the top corners meet the circle.

Analysis

A circle with its center at the center of the page governs the placement of the figure and the type, "JOB." The upper right to lower left diagonal visually organizes the placement of the head, eye, and hand. The upper left to lower right diagonal flows through the shoulder and past the hip.

Bauhaus Ausstellung Poster, Fritz Schleifer, 1922

Fritz Schleifer celebrated the tenants of Constructivism in his 1922, *Bauhaus Ausstellung* (Bauhaus Exhibition) poster. As per the Constructivist ideals of the time, the human profile and the typography are abstracted into simple geometric shapes of the mechanical machine age.

The geometric face, originally designed as part of a Bauhaus seal by Oskar Schlemmer, is further reduced from Schlemmer's original to five simple rectangular shapes by eliminating the fine horizontal and vertical lines. The width of the smallest rectangle, the mouth, is the module of measure for the width of the other rectangles.

The typography is designed to be consistent with the same rectangular elements as the face. It echoes the rigid angular forms. The typeface is similar to an original face designed by Théo van Doesburg in 1920.

48

Bauhaus Seal, Oskar Schlemmer, 1922

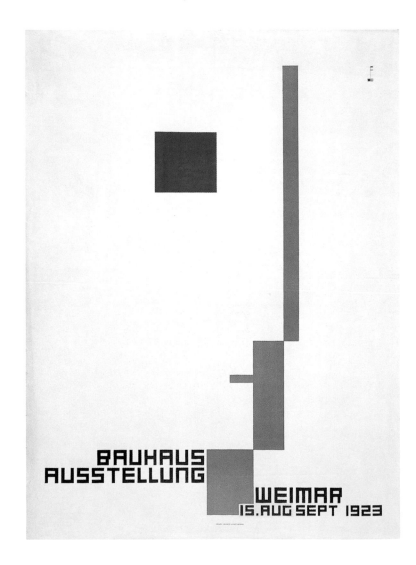

Type Design

The type structure is based on a 5 unit by 5 unit square, which permits the widest characters, M and W, to occupy a full square with each stroke and counterform occupying a unit. The narrower characters occupy a 5 X 4 portion of the square, again with each stroke occupying a unit and the counterforms enlarged to two units. The B and R deviate in that a concession of 1/2 unit is made to the rounded forms and to distinguish the R from the A and the B from the number 8.

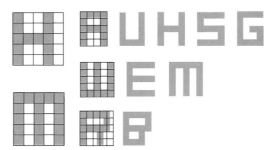

Analysis

The eye aligns along the center vertical axis. The other facial elements are placed in asymmetric relationship to this axis. The type aligns top and bottom with the neck rectangle.

Rectangle Width Proportion

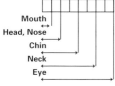

Mouth
Head, Nose
Chin
Neck
Eye

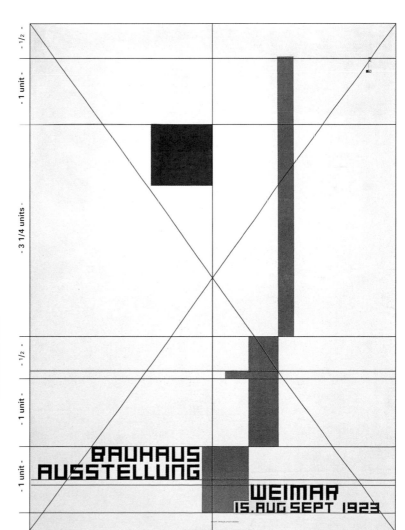

49

L'Intransigéant Poster, A. M. Cassandre, 1925

"The mathematically expressed module can only act to confirm a spontaneous insight. The golden rule merely defines the ideal proportion previously intuited by the artist; it is a means of verifying, not a system (it would be doomed [if it were], like every system)."

Diary, Adolphe Mouron, 1960

The *L'Intransigéant* poster designed in 1925 by Adolphe Mouron, who was more widely known as A. M. Cassandre, is both a conceptual triumph and a study in geometric construction. The poster is for a Parisian newspaper, *L'Intransigéant*, and the conceptual triumph is the translation of the representational form of a woman's head into the visual symbol of Marianne, the voice of France.

Cassandre was educated as an artist and studied painting at a number of studios in Paris. Indeed, he took the pseudonym Cassandre with the idea that

50

when he returned to painting that he would do so under his given name, Adolphe Mouron. Very soon, however, he became fascinated by poster art and found that it held more potential for dynamic experimentation than did painting for him. The idea of mass communication was appealing as well as the idea of an art that crossed the traditional and entrenched boundaries of class distinction.

Because of his interest and studies in painting, Cassandre was deeply influenced by Cubism. In an interview in 1926 he described Cubism: "...its relentless logic and the artist's endeavors to construct his work geometrically bring out the eternal element, the impersonal element beyond all contingencies and individual complexities." He acknowledged that his work was "essentially geometric and monumental," and the elements of geometric construction can be

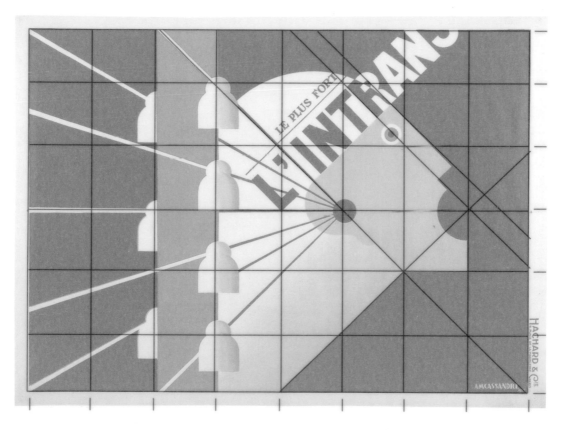

Analysis

The poster format is organized into a series of modules 6 X 8, yielding a total of 48 square visual fields. All elements of the poster correspond to this plan in terms of placement and proportion. The inner ear is at the intersection of these visual fields as is the center of the mouth. The corner of the "L" lands in the exact center of the poster. The chin of the figure fits into a visual field, as does the telegraph pole. The 45° angle of the neck moves from corner to corner of a square of four visual fields. The telegraph wires begin at the ear center and move at 15° increments forming again 45° angles above and below the horizontal.

found in almost all of his posters. In particular Cassandre was very conscious of the compelling visual power of the circle and consciously used the circle in this poster and many other posters to direct and focus the viewer's attention.

In addition to fine-art Cubism, the poster movement called Sach Plakat, or the object poster, influenced Cassandre's work. The object poster movement departed from the expressive and embellished work of the past with objectivity and function as the primary goals. This philosophy was echoed by the Bauhaus in the 1920s and can be seen repeatedly in Cassandre's posters throughout his career. In *L'Intrans* the newspaper is reduced to a just a portion of the masthead that overlaps a more powerful symbol, Marianne, the voice of France.

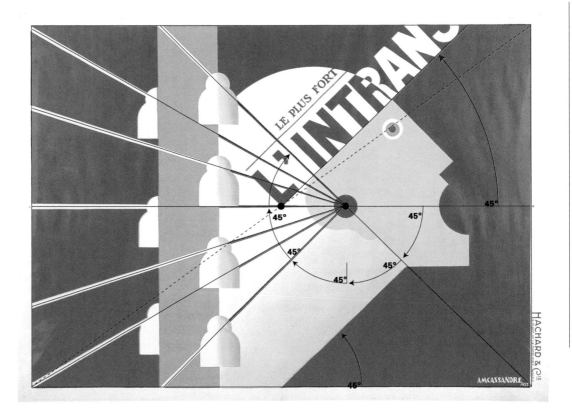

Angles and Root 2

The format of the poster is a root 2 rectangle. The eye is bisected by the diagonal of the root 2 rectangle, shown with a dashed line. This diagonal also bisects the center of the poster at the lower left corner of the "L." The baseline of the word, L'INTRANS, is at a 45° diagonal from the center of the poster. The telegraph wire lines are arranged at approximately 15° increments which yield the 45° module that is repeated in the nose and neck angles.

Circle Diameter Ratios

head circle	= 4 mouth circles
mouth circle	= outer ear circle
mouth circle	= 2 1/2 small ear circles
inner ear circle	= eye circle
inner ear circle	= insulator circles
inner ear circle	= ear lobe circle

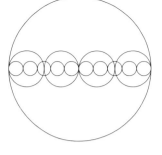

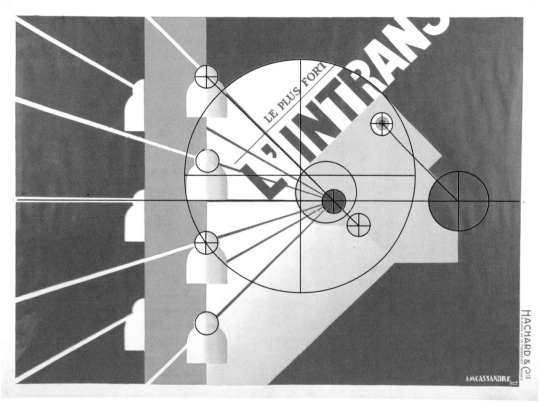

Circle Proportions

The outer ear and mouth circles are the diameter of one visual field. The smaller circles of the eye, inner ear, ear lobe, and insulator have a diameter of two fifths of a visual field, The largest circle, the head, has a diameter of four visual fields.

The placement of the circles is organized so that the center points of circles on the head are aligned on 45° diagonals. The insulator circles are all aligned on diagonals at approximately 15° increments. Three of these 15° increments yield the 45° module.

East Coast by L.N.E.R. Poster, Tom Purvis, 1925

Tom Purvis' 1925 poster, *East Coast by L.N.E.R.*, is an invitation to the viewer for summer vacation travel on the London Northeast Railroad. More than twenty-five years earlier two designers who called themselves the Begarstaffs experimented with the then radical approach of developing powerful compositions of flat areas of color defining simplified graphic silhouettes. Purvis' poster uses a similar technique of simplification and play of space, color, and pattern.

The umbrella ellipse is the most powerful and compelling visual force in the poster, not only because of the vibrant color but also because of the shape and diagonal placement. The bright orange is in complimentary contrast to the blue sky and water. The elliptical shape is close to the shape of the circle, which attracts more visual attention than any other geometric form. The diagonal direction is the most provoking visual direction due to its instability

and implied motion. The dramatic ellipse is repeated two more times in the interior structure of the umbrella and in the black pole support.

All of the shapes are simple silhouette shapes created with great economy of detail. The striped texture and casual arrangement of the towel provides a change in texture from the simple shapes.

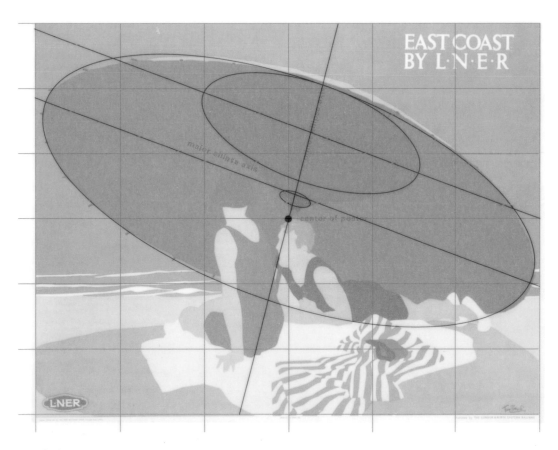

Analysis

The poster is readily analyzed by means of a 6 X 6 grid. The horizon line of the sky and water divides the poster and occupies the top two thirds. The minor ellipse axis of the orange umbrella passes through the center of the poster and balances the composition. The figures rest left and right of this axis, providing a balance of color and shape.

Barcelona Chair, Mies van der Rohe, 1929

The *Barcelona Chair* was designed in 1929 for the German Pavilion at the International Exhibition in Barcelona, Spain. The pavilion was unlike any of the others in that it did not contain any exhibits; the building itself was the exhibit. Elegant, sparse, and consisting of travertine marble, gray glass, chrome columns, and dark green marble, the building's only furnishings were *Barcelona Chairs* and *Barcelona Ottomans* upholstered in white leather, and *Barcelona Tables*. The ottomans and tables used a support "x" frame similar to the chair. Mies van der Rohe designed the building and the furniture, and both are considered milestones of design as well as the greatest achievement of van der Rohe's European career.

It's difficult to believe that such a contemporary, classical piece was designed and produced more than seventy years ago. The *Barcelona* Chair is a symphony of meticulous proportions based on a simple

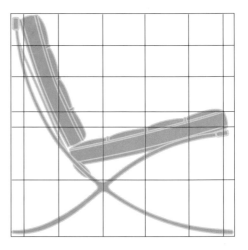

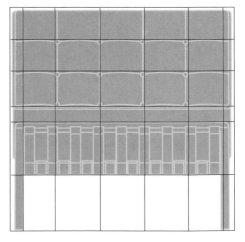

Chair Proportions (right)
The chair side view (top right) as well as front view (bottom right) fit perfectly into a square. The divisions of the back cushion approximate small root 2 rectangles.

56

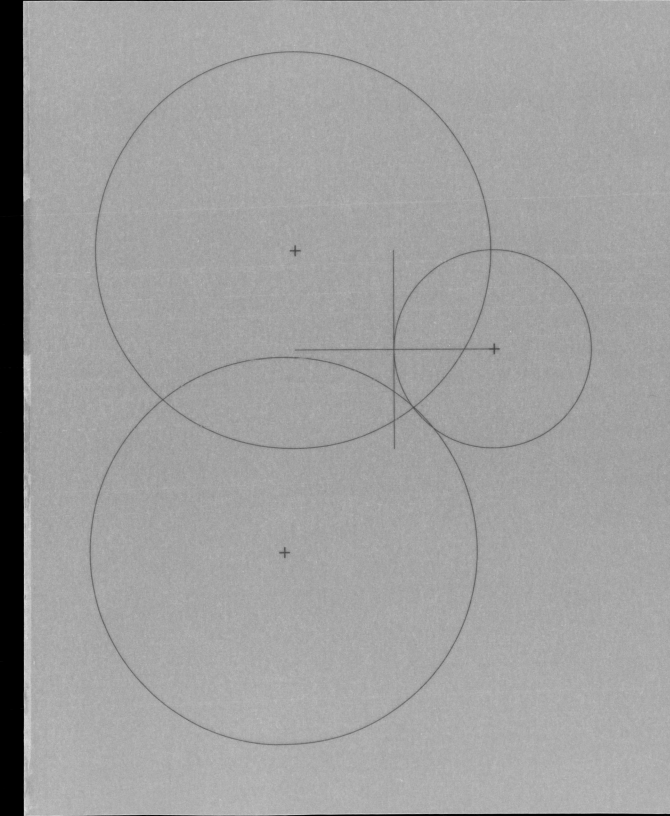

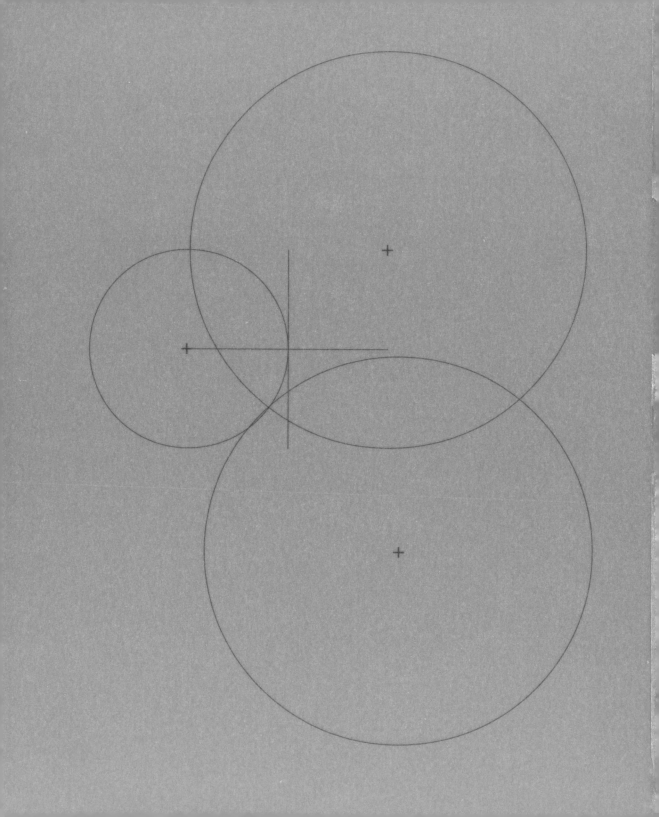

square. The height of the chair is equal to the length which is equal to the depth, i.e. it fits perfectly into a cube. The rectangles of leather on the cushions are in root 2 rectangle proportion attached to a steel frame. The same rectangles were designed so that when the chair was upholstered they would still be perfect rectangles despite the stress and tension of the upholstery process. The script "x" construction of the legs form an elegant frame and lasting trademark for the chair.

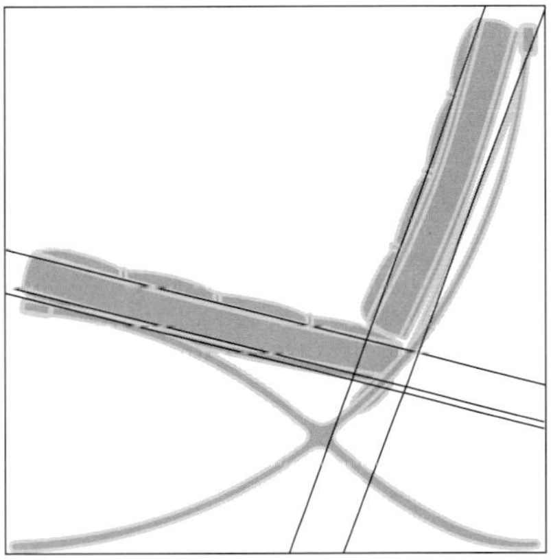

A

C

B

57

Curve Proportions
The primary curve of the chair back and front leg is formed by a circle with the same radius as the square, with center point A. The curve of the original circle is repeated on the front of the seat support with an identical circle with center point B. Another circle, with one-half the radius of the first, defines the back leg with center point C.

Chaise Longue, Le Corbusier, 1929

Architects educated in the Beaux Arts tradition often are very aware of the principles of classic proportion, and involve these principles both in the architecture and furniture that they design. Le Corbusier is one of these architects and the attention to detail and proportion in his architecture can also be found in his *Chaise Longue.* Corbusier was influenced in the 1920s by other architects such as Mies van der Rohe who were designing tubular steel furniture for their buildings. Both Corbusier and Mies were influenced by the geometric forms of Thonet Bentwood furniture and used simplified similar forms in their own work.

In 1927, Le Corbusier began a collaboration with Charlotte Perriand, a furniture and interior designer, and his cousin, Pierre Jeanneret. The collaboration was highly successful and lead to a number of classic furniture designs that bear Le Corbusier's name, including the *Chaise Longue.*

58

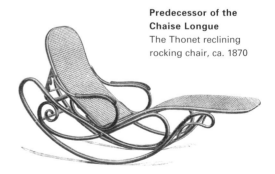

Predecessor of the Chaise Longue
The Thonet reclining rocking chair, ca. 1870

The chrome tubular frame of the Chaise is an arc runner that rests on simple black stand. This arc is an elegantly simple system that slides in either direction and allows the user an infinite variety of positions, and is held in place by friction and gravity with either the head or feet raised. Similar to the geometric arc frame, the pillow is also a geometric form of a cylinder that is easily repositioned by the user. The arc of the frame is such that the frame can be removed from the stand and used as a reclining rocker.

Analysis

The proportions of the chaise relate to the harmonic subdivisions of a golden rectangle. The width of the rectangle becomes the diameter of the arc that is the frame of the chaise. The stand is in direct relationship to the square in the harmonic subdivision. The Chaise Longue is analyzed by a harmonic decomposition of a golden section rectangle.

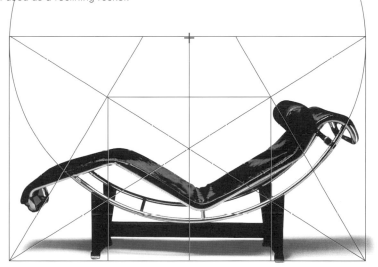

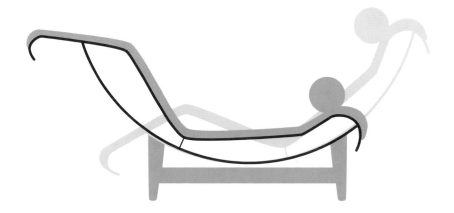

Brno Chair, Mies van der Rohe, 1929

Mies van der Rohe received a commission to design a family residence for the Tugendhat family based on his highly acclaimed architecture for the Barcelona Pavilion in 1929. In addition, he was asked to design furniture for the residence that would be in keeping with the stark modernism of the building.

Mies had successfully developed a cantilever armchair, the MR Chair, in 1926. At the time the technology of bending tubular steel was new and presented innovative design options. The design of the MR Chair was based on earlier nineteenth-century designs of tubular iron rockers and the celebrated Bentwood Rocker by Michael Thonet. Because of the strength of tubular steel the frame of the MR Chair was cantilevered and the design simplified.

The Tugendhat house had a large dining room and a table that could seat 24. The MR Chair was originally specified for this purpose but was awkward as a

Predecessors of the Brno Chair
(left) Thonet Bentwood Rocker, ca. 1860, (right) side view of the MR Chair, Mies van der Rohe, 1926

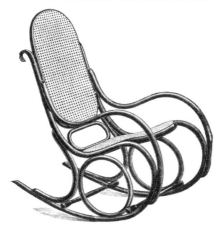

dining chair because the extended arms did not fit under the table. The Brno Chair, named after the town of Brno where the Tugendhats lived, was designed for this purpose and the low sweep of the arms and compact form fit neatly under a dining table. The original chairs were upholstered in leather and the design was executed in both tubular steel and flat bar versions, which resulted in structural variations.

Analysis

The chair top view fits perfectly into a square (above right).The front view of the chair (right) and side view (far right) fit neatly into a golden section rectangle. The angle of the front legs and chair back (below right) are symmetrical, and the radii of the curves are in 1:3 proportion.

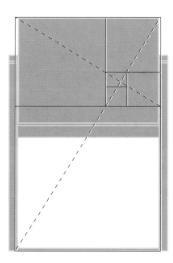

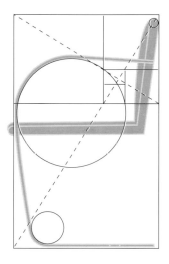

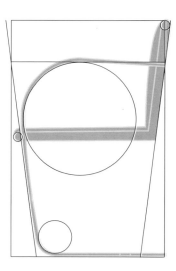

Negerkunst Poster, Max Bill, 1931

This poster was for an exhibition of South African pre-historic rock painting. The fierce simplicity and geometry of Max Bill's 1931 *Negerkunst* poster have roots in the development of the Art Concrete ideal of the 1930s. This movement demanded arithmetical construction of pure visual elements. Bill embraced this ideal as a universal visual language of absolute clarity.

The diameter of the center circle becomes the key measure for the entire figure. The measure of the diameter is the same as the height of the top and bottom. Half of this diameter is the measure of the sides. The vertical that pierces the center of the circle becomes the axis for the left edge of the type.

62

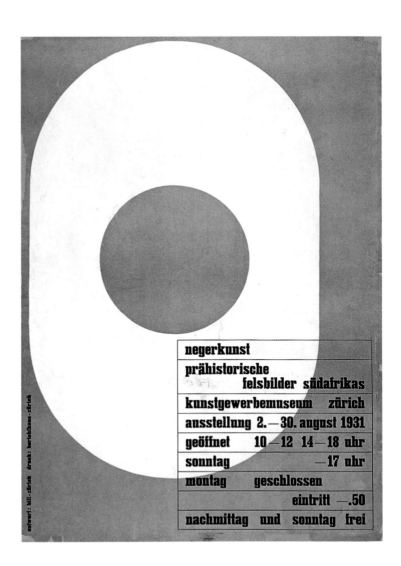

Large Circle Proportions (right)

The exterior circles are two times the size of the interior circle.

Root 2 Proportions (far right)

The format of the poster is based on a root 2 rectangle. The diagram is a harmonic decomposition of a root 2 rectangle. The vertical line becomes the axis for the block of type and the center of the interior circle.

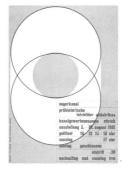

Analysis

The proportions of the large "O" are based on a module of the interior circle. The left and right sides are one-half the diameter of the interior circle and the top and bottom sides are the measure of one diameter of the interior circle. The corner to corner diagonal pierces the center of the interior circle, and a vertical through the center determines the left margin of the type box.

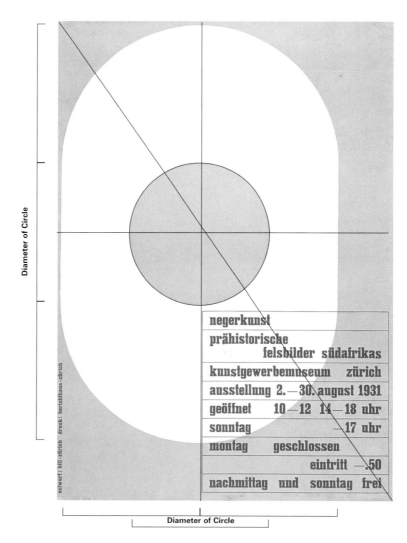

Diameter of Circle

Diameter of Circle

63

Wagon-Bar Poster, A. M. Cassandre, 1932

"Some people call my posters Cubistic. They are right in the sense that my method is essentially geometric and monumental. Architecture, which I prefer above all others, has taught me to abhor distorting idiosyncrasies... I have always been more sensitive to forms than to colors, to the way things are organized than to their details, to the spirit of geometry than to the spirit of refinement..."

Adolphe Mouron, A. M. Cassandre, *La Revue de l'Union de l'Affiche Française*, 1926

The *Wagon-Bar* Poster is no less a marvel of geometric interrelationships than is the earlier *L'Intrans*. Again, Cassandre selects representational elements to be simplified and stylized into simple geometric forms. The seltzer bottle, wine and water glasses, loaf of bread, wine bottle, and straws are placed in front of a photograph of a train wheel.

The diameter of the wheel becomes the measure of the railroad track segment that emphasizes,

"RESTAUREZ-VOUS," and "A PEU DE FRAIS." The center of the poster is visually punctuated by the ends of the two straws in the drinking glass. The poster is easily divided into thirds on the vertical.

The geometry of the drawn imagezs is apparent in the shoulders of the bottles and the bowl of the wine glass. There is a beautiful play of space as the white background of the poster bleeds into the siphon top of the seltzer bottle. A similar change of space occurs

with the bread loaf and the wine bottle label as well as the top of the glass and the edge of the wheel casing.

This poster is relatively complex in the number of elements that require geometric simplification, structural interrelationships, and organizational control. Yet upon analysis it is clear that there is a reason for each and every decision.

Analysis

Conscious placement and control of each element is evident in the center points of the circles that form the wine glass bowl and the shoulders of the seltzer bottle as they land on the diagonal from the upper left corner to lower right corner. Likewise, the center of the wine bottle circle and the wheel center align on the same vertical.

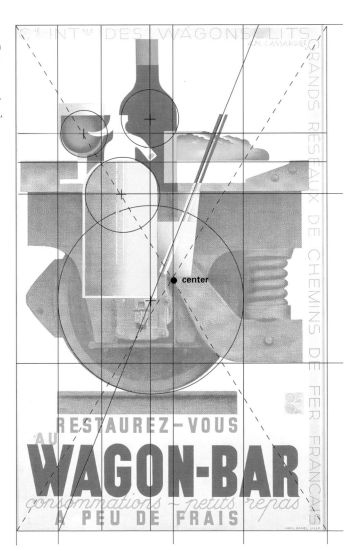

Konstruktivisten Poster, Jan Tschichold, 1937

"We do not know why, but we can demonstrate that a human being finds planes of definite and intentional proportions more pleasant or more beautiful than those of accidental proportions."
Jan Tschichold, *The Form of the Book*, 1975

This poster, created by Jan Tschichold in 1929, was for an exhibition of Constructivist art. Since this poster was created at a time when the Constructivist movement was dissipating, the circle and line can be interpreted as a setting sun. The Constructivist art movement mechanized fine art and graphic design via mathematical placement of abstracted geometric elements as a functional expression of industrial culture. As a poster, this work utilizes the Constructivist ideals of geometric abstraction, mathematical visual organization, and asymmetric typography as advocated in Tschichold's book, *Die Neue Typographie*, published in 1928.

66

Analysis

The diameter of the circle becomes a unit of measurement for the poster and placement of the elements. The circle itself is a focal point and the eye is inexorably pulled toward it. The circle also highlights the title of the exhibition as well as the list of exhibitors. The small bullet circle next to the line of text with the dates of the exhibition is an element of visual punctuation as it echoes to and contrasts in scale with the major circle. The list of exhibition contributors begins at the meeting point of the diagonals of the poster format and the diagonal of the bottom rectangular section. The distances of the text to major elements are modules of the distance from the horizontal line to the base line of "konstruktivisten," which is centered in the circle.

Compositional Triangle

The typography of the poster forms a triangle which serves to anchor it to the format and enhance visual interest.

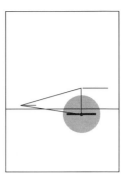

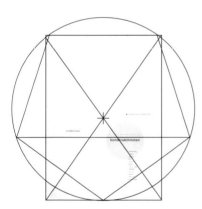

Format Proportions

The narrow rectangular format is a pentagram page and is derived from a pentagon inscribed in a circle. The top surface of the pentagon becomes the width of the rectangle and the bottom point the bottom of the rectangle. The horizontal line in the poster is placed so as to connect two of the vertices of the pentagon.

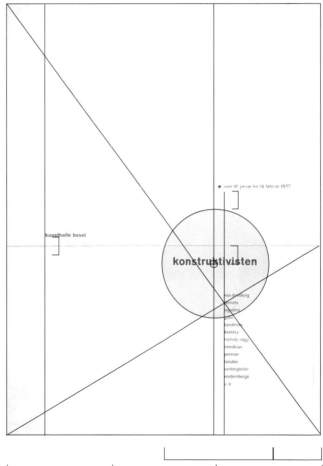

Der Berufsphotograph Poster, Jan Tschichold, 1938

This 1938 poster by Jan Tschichold was for an exhibition of the work of professional photographers and is a classic in concept and composition after many decades. Because of the exhibition content, the image of a woman is representational but also abstracted in that she is portrayed as a film negative. This technique focuses the viewer's attention on the process of photography rather than on a single image of a woman. The main title, "der berufsphotograph," is printed as a split font, whereby three different colors of ink, yellow, red, and blue are placed on a printing roller and "mix" as the roller turns. This rainbow of color in the typography is a rare expressionist departure from the formalism of Tschichold's other work. However, his love of asymmetric and functional typography are evident in the layout of carefully aligned and related typographic elements and textures.

unter mitarbeil des schweizerischen photographen-verbandes

gewerbemuseum basel   ausstellung

der berufsphotograph   seine arbeiten — sein werkzeug

8. mai — 6. juni

	werktags	14-19	
	mittwochs	14-19	19-21
	sonntags	10-12	14-19
	eintritt frei		

Root 2 Rectangle Relationships

The root 2 construction diagram is placed on top of the poster. The corner of the reciprocal and the diagonals bisect the eye of the figure in the photograph.

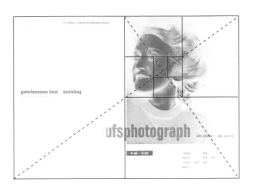

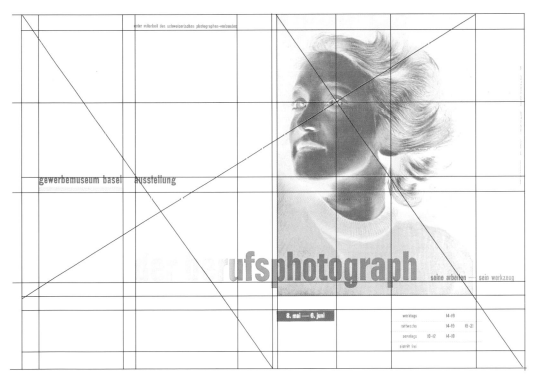

center line

69

Analysis

The negative photograph is just to the right of the center of the root 2 rectangle format. The left eye of the figure is carefully placed and the image cropped so as to become the nexus of diagonals that regulate the placement of elements. The measure of the width and depth of the image is echoed by the typographic elements to the left.

Plywood Chair, Charles Eames, 1946

Although he had a full scholarship to study architecture, Charles Eames left college after two years at Washington University in St. Louis. The curriculum was based on the traditional principles of the Academy of the Beaux Arts, which clashed with his avid interest in modernism and the work of Frank Lloyd Wright. However, throughout his life he appreciated the foundation that the Beaux Arts training had given him in the classical principles of proportion and architecture.

His *Plywood Chair* was designed for an Organic Furniture Competition sponsored by the Museum of Modern Art in 1940. Eames and his collaborator architect Eero Saarinen sought to bring organic forms together into a unified whole. As a result the beautiful curvilinear forms caught the eye of the judges, as did the innovative technologies of three-dimensional molded plywood and a new rubber weld technique that joined the plywood to metal. The entry won first place.

Plywood Chair
(above) All plywood version and (right) plywood and metal version. The chair was made in two versions; a lower lounge chair version and a slightly higher dining chair version.

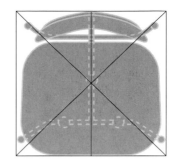

The current chair, still in production, evolved from that winning entry. It is impossible to state unequivocally that the relationship of the chair's proportions to the golden section rectangle were fully consciously planned, but the classical Beaux Arts training, as well as the collaboration with Eero Saarinen, make this assumption highly likely.

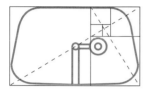

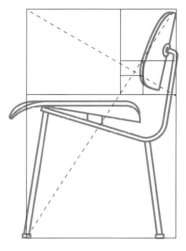

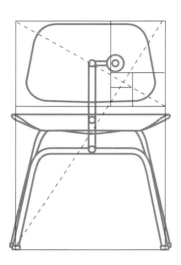

Chair Back (above)
The chair back fits perfectly into a golden section rectangle.

Chair Proportions (right)
The dining chair proportions are roughly those of the golden section.

Chair Detail Proportions
The radii of the corners of the chair back as well as the tubular legs are in proportion to each other 1:4:6:8.

A= 1
B= 4
C= 6
D= 8

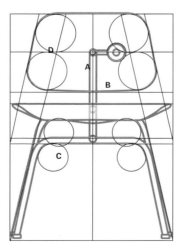

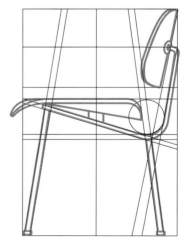

Konkrete Kunst Poster, Max Bill, 1944

"I am of the opinion that it is possible to develop an art largely on the basis of mathematical thinking."
Max Bill, from an interview in 1949, *Typographic Communications Today*, 1989

Max Bill was distinguished as a fine artist, architect, and typographer. He studied at the Bauhaus under Walter Gropius, Moholy-Nagy, and Josef Albers among others. At the Bauhaus he was influenced by the ideals of functionalism, the De Stijl style, and for-

mal mathematical organization. The hallmarks of the 1920s De Stijl style included a very formal dividing of space with horizontal and vertical lines. This style had softened by the time this work was created in 1944. The space is divided but with a circle and arcs, and the rigid horizontal lines of some De Stijl typefaces are evolved to include circles and diagonals.

Bill's use of geometric abstraction was developed to include the typographic elements as well. The letter

Root 2 Construction (right)

Root 2 construction relates directly to the placement of the circles. The diagonal pierces the centers of the largest and smallest circles, and the smallest circle rests on the line of the root 2 construction square.

Circle Proportions (far right)

The proportion of the circles is 1:3:6.

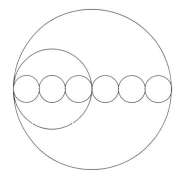

Analysis

The diameter of the smallest circle is 1/3 the poster width as well as 1/3 the diameter of the next largest circle, and 1/6 the diameter of the largest circle. The smallest type has an alignment with the smallest circle and the larger type aligns with the circle tangent and edge of the smallest circle.

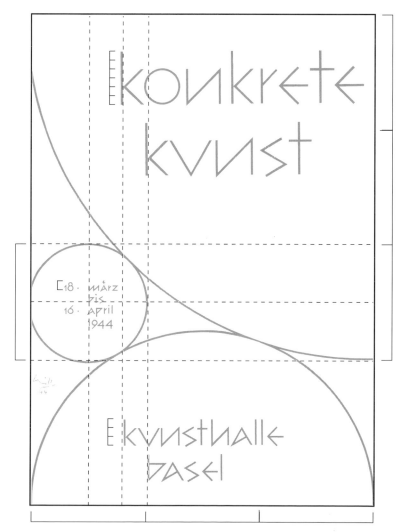

73

forms are hand generated and based on the same root 2 principle as the poster format. Each typographic character has a direct geometric relationship to the structure of the root 2 rectangle and is created in modular form. The font was used for other posters and also for an exhibit that Bill designed in 1949.

Type Construction
The construction square of the rectangle is the base line and mean line or x-height of the lowercase font. The ascenders and descenders are defined by the length of the root 2 rectangle. The strokes are based on geometric construction with angles restrained to 45°. Deviation of the angles occurs in the "s" with 30° and 60° construction, and in the major strokes of the "a" and "v" with 63° angles. Two root two rectangles are used to create the "m" which is two repeated "n" shapes. The numbers are created with the same construction methods, utilizing a perfect circle, which reflects the larger circle shapes in the composition.

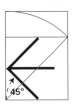

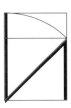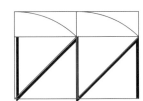

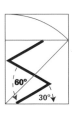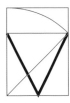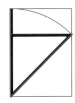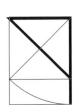

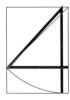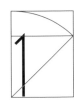

Letter Form Size Proportions

The letter forms are of a single weight and the same proportion as the circles, 1:3:6.

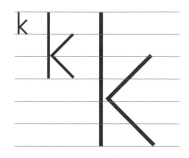

Pevsner, Vantongerloo, Bill Poster, Max Bill, 1949

This poster designed four years after *Konkrete Kunst*, uses the same letter form construction. Bill later slightly refined the letter form construction for use in an exhibition, and this face is currently available from The Foundry in London.

Illinois Institute of Technology Chapel,
Mies van der Rohe, 1949-1952

Mies van der Rohe is best known for his monumental architecture of steel and glass skyscrapers. He was a master of proportioning systems and many of these skyscrapers are so similar in form and proportion that they can be classified as a single archetype. Mies was the Director of the School of Architecture at the Illinois Institute of Technology for twenty years, and during that time he designed the entire campus and many of the buildings on it.

The IIT chapel is a good example of his use of proportioning on a smaller scale. The entire building façade is in the proportion of a golden section, 1:1.618, or roughly 3:5. The building is also perfectly subdivided into five columns by golden rectangles, and when those rectangles are repeated in a pattern, the building is a module of 5 X 5 horizontal rectangles.

76

Illinois Institute of Technology Chapel
(above) Exterior view of the front façade.
(right) Interior view.

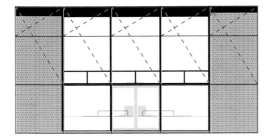

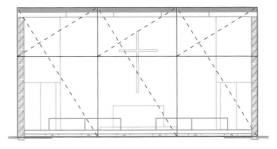

Golden Section Proportions

The golden section proportion can readily be seen in these drawings. (top left) The front façade of the chapel can be subdivided into a series of golden section rectangles that surround the top large windows and smaller top hung ventilator windows. The bottom large windows are squares. (top right) The section drawing of the interior looking towards the altar shows that the perimeter of the front façade can be defined by three golden section rectangles. (below right) The plan of the chapel perimeter fits perfectly into a golden section rectangle. The square of the golden section rectangle defines the area for the congregation and the reciprocal golden section rectangle defines the altar and service and storage areas of the chapel. These two areas are separated by a small elevation of the altar area and railing. The original plan of the chapel had no seating; however, seating was added later.

The photograph at left is from the 1950's. Sadly, in recent years this building has suffered from inaccurate window replacement and poor repair. Visitors to the site should not expect to find the building as shown.

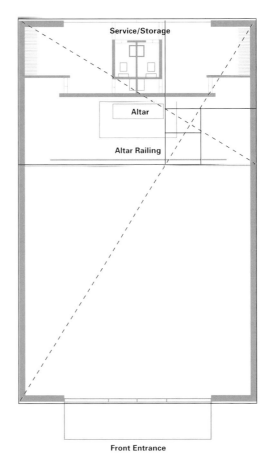

Service/Storage

Altar

Altar Railing

Front Entrance

77

Beethoven Poster, Josef Müller-Brockmann, 1955

"The proportions of the formal elements and their intermediate spaces are almost always related to certain numerical progressions logically followed out."

Josef Müller-Brockmann, *The Graphic Artist and His Design Problems*, 1961

Josef Müller-Brockmann, is known as one of the founders of the Swiss or International Style. His Tonhalle concert posters during the 1940s and 1950s were pivotal in setting a standard for grid system visual organization.

As a conceptual work the geometric rhythms of the concentric circle arcs relate directly to the mathematical systems and structures present in music. As a structured work of design, every element has a reason for its size, placement, and position. The dramatic change in the proportion of the concentric circle arcs echoes the drama of Beethoven's music.

All of Josef Müller-Brockmann's work can be geometrically analyzed in a similar manner. The use of a mathematical plan, logically constructed, is always employed in his work.

Analysis

The center of the circle is at the upper left edge of the body text. All angles extend from the center of this circle. Angles are based on a module of 45°. The smallest angles are 1/4 of the module or 11.25°, the next largest are 22.5°, and then 45°.

As the circle arcs rotate around the center point they vary in width from one unit to thirty-two units–doubling the width in a progression.

The flush left text block and corresponding vertical angle provide an axis, as does the horizontal top of the text block and its corresponding horizontal angle.

Angle Organization (near right)

The planned proportion and placement of the angles is readily seen when a square is inscribed in the first circle.

Root 2 Structure (far right)

The format of the poster is based on a root 2 rectangle as per the overlay root 2 construction diagram. The center of the circles is placed on the bottom of the construction square.

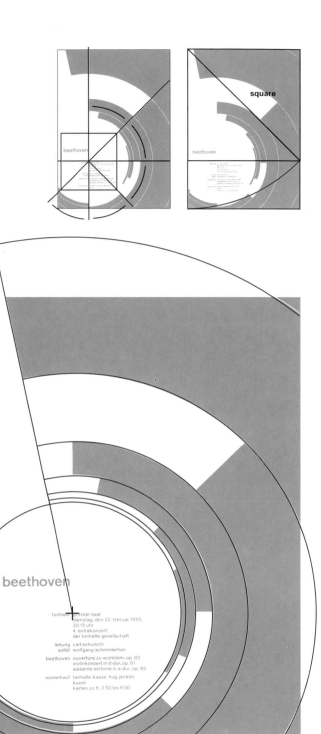

Arc Proportion

The width of the circle arcs vary from one unit to thirty-two units. Each arc is double the width of the previous 1, 2, 4, 8, 16, 32. The broadest arc of thirty-two units is only hinted at with a segment division in the upper right corner of the poster.

Original Production Drawing

Below is the original production drawing by Josef Müller-Brockmann.

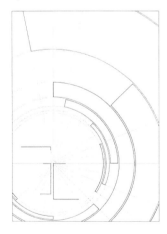

beethoven

tonhalle grosser saal
dienstag, den 22. februar 1955,
20.15 uhr
4. extrakonzert
der tonhalle-gesellschaft

leitung   carl schuricht
solist   wolfgang schneiderhan

beethoven ouverture zu «coriolan», op. 62
violinkonzert in d-dur, op. 61
siebente sinfonie in a-dur, op. 92

vorverkauf tonhalle-kasse, hug, jecklin,
kuoni
karten zu fr. 3.50 bis 9.50

Musica Viva **Poster, Josef Müller-Brockmann, 1957**

This is a poster from the extensive Tonhalle series by Josef Müller-Brockmann. During the 1950's he was testing his theories of constructive graphic design, based on constructed geometric elements without illustration or embellishment. Each poster in the series uses a geometric form, such as rectangles, squares, circles, arcs, as a visual theme. The compositions are carefully controlled with planned rhythms and repetitions of elements.

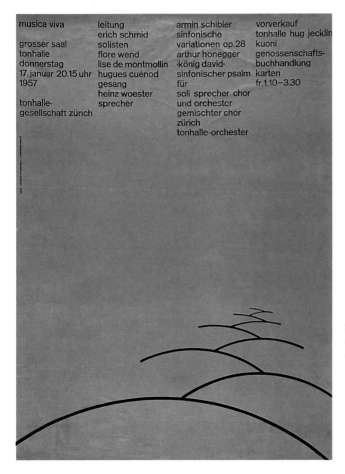

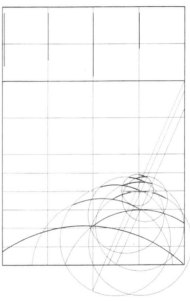

Production Diagram
(above) The original production diagram for the poster.

Musica Viva Poster, Josef Müller-Brockmann, 1958

This Müller-Brockmann poster is from the Tonhalle series and, as with all of his work, is based on geometric planning. The repetitive non-objective elements are circles and the play is in the spaces and proportion. Each circle is 2 1/2 times the size of the next smallest circle. This can be seen in the diagram as the next smaller circle occupies one quadrant.

The image portion of the format is defined by a root 2 rectangle, which is determined by dropping an arc from the top horizontal edge of the poster. The bottom of this edge becomes the horizontal center line of the second smallest circle. Vertical lines from the center of the circles align with columns and in the case of the largest circle align with the edge of the format.

82

dienstag, den 7. januar 1958
20.15 uhr großer tonhallesaal
12. volkskonzert
der tonhalle-gesellschaft
zürich
als drittes konzert
im zyklus «musica viva»
leitung hans rosbaud
solisten alfred baum klavier
andré jaunet flöte

schweizerische erstaufführungen
andré jolivet
cinque danses rituelles
ernst krenek
zweites klavierkonzert
luigi nono
«y su sangre va vienne cantando»
musik für flöte und kleines orchester
bernd aloys zimmermann
sinfonie in einem satz

musica viva

karten fr. 1.-, 2.- und 3.-
vorverkauf tonhallekasse hug
jecklin kuoni
genossenschaftsbuchhandlung

Root 2 Construction and Circle Positions

This poster format is based on the root 2 rectangle as per the construction diagram in black line. The bottom edge of the square pierces the third largest circle center and is the base line for the second largest circle. The dashed black line of the construction diagonal separates the two largest circles.

Circle Proportions

The circles are in proportion to each other in a ratio of 2: 5.

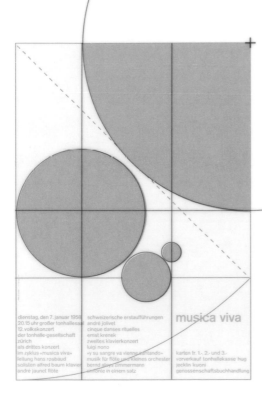

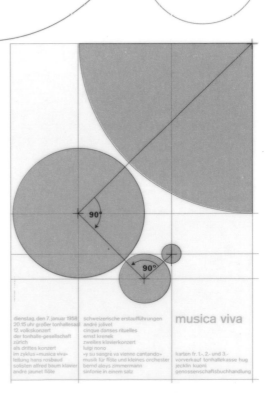

Analysis

The placement of the circles is determined by the diagonal of the square, and the circle centers are arranged at 90° angles to each other. The x-height of the "*musica viva*" type is in proportion to the smallest circle, 1:1.41. This is root 2 proportion. The column widths are determined by the edges and centers of the circles.

Pedestal Chair, Eero Saarinen, 1957

Eero Saarinen's love of simplicity and unified forms can be seen in his architecture, such as the Gateway Arch in St. Louis, Missouri, as well as in his furniture design of the *Pedestal Group*. Saarinen had collaborated earlier with Charles Eames on the design of the *Plywood Chair* and his quest for truly unified organic forms was brought to fruition with the Pedestal Group in 1957.

Saarinen sought to simplify interiors and eliminate what he considered the disarray of table and chair legs. The forms were so sleek, modern, and unexpected that they became icons of the future.

The side chair version of the *Pedestal Group* is shown here and is part of a group that includes stools, arm chairs, and side tables. The front and side views of the chair fit comfortably into golden section proportions and the pedestal curves bear a relationship to the golden section ellipse.

Golden Ellipse

Similar to the golden rectangle, the ratio of the major axis to the minor axis of the golden ellipse is 1:1.62. There is also evidence that the human cognitive preference is with an ellipse of these proportions.

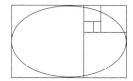

Analysis

The front view of the chair fits easily into golden section proportions (far right). The front view can also be analyzed as two overlapping squares; the bottom square meeting the top of the seat cushion and the top square meeting the joint of the pedestal to the seat.

The major chair pedestal curves to conform readily to the golden ellipse proportions at both the top and bottom.

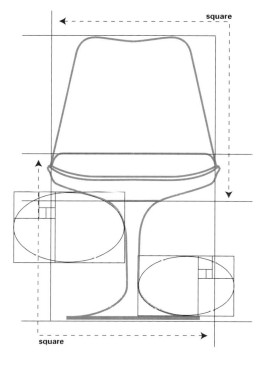

Side and Front Views

Both the side (right) and front views (far right) of the pedestal chair fit comfortably into a golden section rectangle. The front lip of the chair is at the center point of the golden rectangle. The base as it attaches to the seat of the chair is about one-third the width.

85

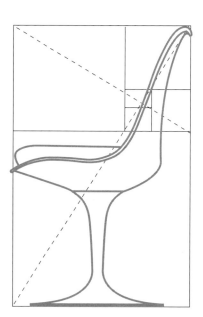

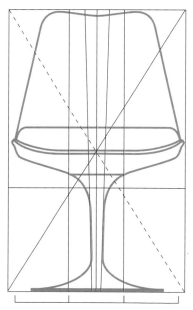

Vormgevers Poster, Wim Crouwel, 1968

This poster was created in 1968, long before the advent of the personal computer. At this time only banks were heavily involved in computer processing and the typeface of this poster has a similar aesthetic to a face of machine-readable numbers found in cheque books. The typography of the poster is both reminiscent of this early computer-readable type and also highly prophetic of the coming digital age. Even then Wim Crouwel envisioned that the screen and computer would play an ever expanding role in typographic communication.

The poster format is in root 2 format, with a square grid pattern, and very simply divided in half. The grid pattern is more complex in that each square is subdivided by a line that is placed one fifth of the distance from the top and right side of the square. The letter forms are "digitally" created, using squares from the grid pattern. The offset grid lines determine the radius of the corners and the same radius is used to link the strokes.

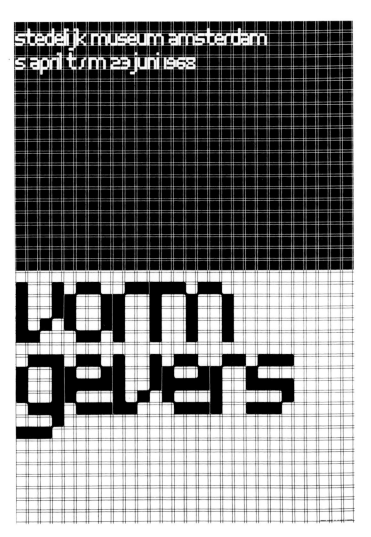

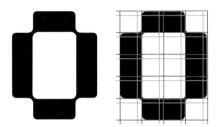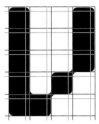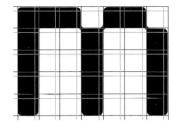

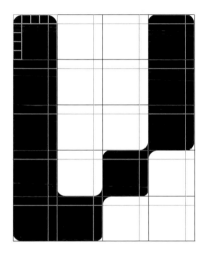

Analysis

The system of construction of the letter
forms is based on the use of a grid shown
in the diagrams with a red line. The
harshness of the square grid is softened
by the use of radii that correspond to offset lines placed 1/5 the distance from the
top and right of each grid square shown
in the diagrams with a gray line. The grid
allows for the "digital" creation of horizontal, vertical, and diagonal strokes. The
alphabet is single case and letters only
have hairline separation in-between. Most
letter forms are created in a 4 X 5 pattern.
Narrow letter forms such as the i and j
only occupy the width of one grid square.
The text at the top of the poster is 1/5 the
size of the text at the bottom.

Fürstenberg Porzellan Poster, Inge Druckery, 1969

Inge Druckery fluidly communicates the fineness and delicacy of Fürstenberg porcelain with this poster. The letter forms are thin, geometric constructions of a single weight, and the curvilinear letter forms, particularly the u and r, are asymmetric compositions of harmony and timeless elegance.

As with most 20th-century European posters this one is in the standard root 2 display format, and the elements have a relationship to root 2 construction. The vertical and horizontal center lines meet as the viewer's eye follows the vertical stroke of the number " 1" as it approaches the apex of the uppercase "A."

Ausstellung der
Werkkunstschule Krefeld
29.11.68 bis 4.1.69

Öffnungszeiten:
Montag - Freitag 10 - 18 Uhr
Samstag 10 - 13 Uhr

221
JAHRE
PORZELLAN
MANU–
FAKTUR
FÜRSTEN–
BERG

Letter Form Construction

The set width of the characters is based on a square divided into thirds. The narrowest letter forms occupy one-third, slightly wider two thirds, and still wider a full square. Finally, four-thirds are used for the widest characters.

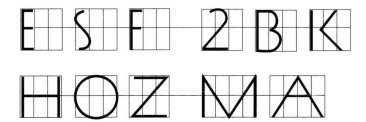

Analysis

The constructed letter forms for "221 JHARE PORZELLAN MANUFAKTUR FÜRSTENBERG" have a height of about 1/16 the depth of the poster. The three lines of the small set type at the top are two-thirds of the depth of the constructed letter forms. The porcelain makers mark, an italic F and crown, is twice the size of the letter-form construction square.

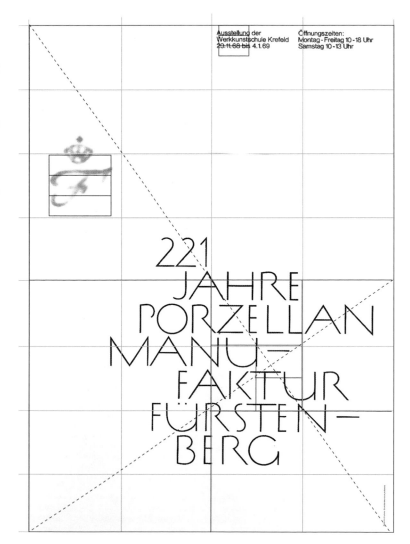

Majakovskij Poster, Bruno Monguzzi, 1975

Bruno Monguzzi recaptures the spirit of the early Russian Constructivists in this poster for an exhibition of work of Russian artists in Milan. The design of this poster reflects the revolutionary ideals of Russian Constructivism of the 1920s. The use of restrained colors, red, black, and gray, and the bold rectangles at a 45° angle give the poster a feeling of visual utilitarianism that was the hallmark of the Constructivists.

Monguzzi uses the same sans serif typography and utilitarian techniques of the Constructivists with a keen compositional eye. Hierarchically, the prominent names of the three artists, Majakovskij, Mejerchol'd, Stanislavskij, are the major visual force. The rules and typography are in the same proportion. A sense of visual space is communicated by the overlapping rules and transparency is created by the red rule overlapping the gray with resulting color change.

Proportional Elements

The width of the rules that the typography is reversed out of is 2:3:4. The typography is synchronized with this proportioning and is also in the proportion of 2:3:4.

Root 2 Format

The circle construction method for the root 2 rectangle reveals the centered "x" that dominates the composition.

Analysis

The three overlapping rules are in a proportion of 2:3:4 and the cap height of the typography follows the same proportional system. A 90° corner of each rule meets the edge of the format to create a strong sense of visual tension.

91

Braun Handblender, 1987

The simple and elegant design of Braun appliances has made them a favorite of artists, architects, and designers. Many pieces are included in the permanent design collection of the Museum of Modern Art. The Braun forms are almost always clean, simple, geometric shapes in white or black with simple controls. The simple lines of the design give each appliance the visual feel of a functional piece of sculpture.

The industrial designers of these three-dimensional works of art employ similar systems and develop similar interrelationships as their graphic design counterparts. Because of the three-dimensional qualities the interrelationships are both visual and structural.

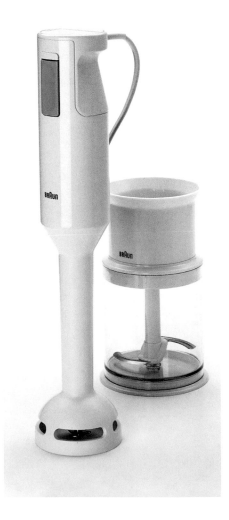

Structure & Proportion

The measure of the long shaft of the handblender is one-third the total height of the appliance. The radii details of the button and surfaces are in concert with each other. There is a symmetry to the surface and even the placement of the corporate name is tightly controlled in relationship to the other elements.

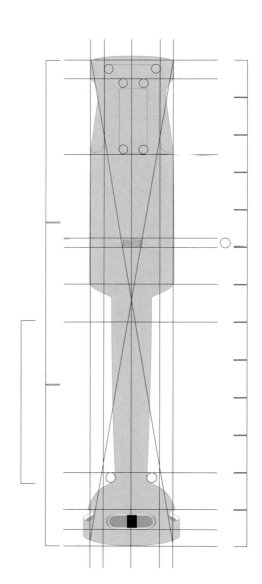

Braun Aromaster Coffee Maker

The Braun coffee maker also has a similar sense of "rightness" to its form. The forms remain geometric and the cylinders are accented by a handle that is almost a pure circle. Again, the corporate name, Braun, is given the same attention to detail, scale, and placement as are all of the other elements. The combination of visual organization of two- and three-dimensional forms causes this appliance to transcend the utilitarian to become a work of sculpture.

Structure & Proportion

The surface of the coffee maker can be divided into a regular series. Each surface element is carefully planned to be in harmony with all others. The logotype, Braun, is slightly above the center. The cylindrical shape of the coffee maker is in keeping with the shape of the handle, which is a segment of a circle. The diagonal of the handle aligns with the top corner. The symmetry of elements can be seen in the fasteners on the switch that align with the measure marks on the pot as well as the center vent opening on the top.

95

Il Conico Kettle, Aldo Rossi, 1980-1983

The Italian design manufacturer, Alessi, has long been known for attracting and producing the work of experimental cutting edge industrial designers. The products are as much art as they are design and so, too, is the *Il Conico* kettle by Aldo Rossi. Rossi's approach is that of a conceptual artist who creates the concept for the product and then turns to the production technicians to resolve production process and details under his direction.

The kettle is a unified composition of geometric solids. The main kettle form is a cone of an equilateral triangle which permits the bottom surface to maximize contact with the heat source and allow for efficient heating. The form of the kettle readily breaks down into a 3 x 3 grid. The top third of the kettle, the vertex, is a delightful small sphere. This sphere makes removing the top easier, but also acts as a form of three-dimensional punctuation for the vertex

of the kettle. The middle third of the kettle consists of the spout and handle. The handle extends out horizontally from the pot and then down vertically. This handle shape can be viewed as an inverted right triangle or a portion of a radius square. All of the primary geometric shapes are part of the composition: cone, triangle, circle, sphere, and square.

Dominant Form

The dominant shape of Il Conico is the cone derived from an equilateral triangle. The handle is an inverted right triangle, one half of an equilateral triangle, and can also be viewed as a portion of a square.

Geometric Structure

The kettle can readily be analyzed with a 3 x 3 grid. The top third is composed of the lid and sphere handle, the middle third the spout and kettle handle, and the wide bottom base permits the maximum contact with the heating surface.

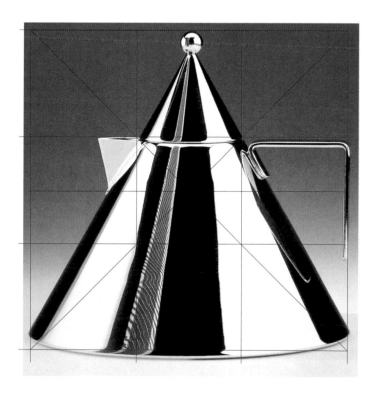

Volkswagen Beetle,
Jay Mays, Freeman Thomas, Peter Schreyer, 1997

The new Volkswagen Beetle is less a vehicle and more a piece of kinetic sculpture as it moves down the road. Distinctly different from other cars, it eloquently captures the visual idea of cohesiveness of form. The body is both part retro and part futuristic, a fusion of geometry and nostalgia.

The body fits neatly into the top half of a golden ellipse. The side windows repeat the shape of the golden ellipse, with the door resting in the square, of the golden section rectangle, and the rear window in the reciprocal golden rectangle. All of the details of changes in surfaces are tangent golden ellipses or circles. Even the placement of the antenna is at an angle tangent to the front wheel well.

Front View

The front of the car is almost square with all surfaces symmetrical. The Volkswagen logo on the hood is at the center of the square.

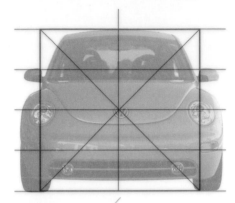

Analysis

A golden ellipse is inscribed in a golden rectangle construction diagram. The body fits cleanly in the top half of this golden ellipse. The major axis of the ellipse aligns with the body just below the center of the tires.
(below) A second golden ellipse encloses the side windows. This ellipse is also tangent to the front wheel well and tangent to the rear wheel. The major axis of the ellipse is tangent to both the front and rear wheel wells.

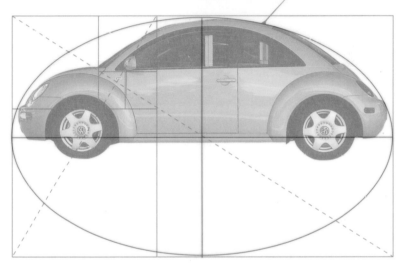

99

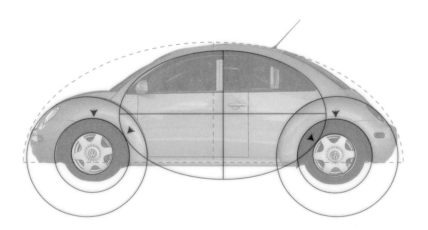

Rear View

Like the front view, the rear view can fit into a square. Again, the logo is near the center point of the square, and all elements and surface changes are symmetrical. The geometry of the car body is also carried through to other details. The headlights and rear lights are ellipses but because they rest on curved surfaces they appear to be circles. Even the door handle is a debossed circle that is bisected by a radiused rectangle with a circular door lock.

Antenna

The angle of the antenna is tangent to the circle of the front wheel fender and the position of the antenna base is aligned with the rear wheel fender.

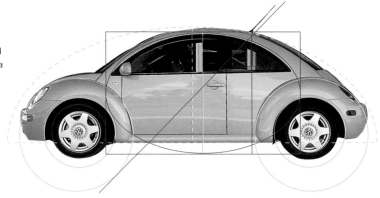

Postscript

Le Corbusier in *The Modulor*, 1949:

"... The regulating lines are not, in principle, a preconceived plan; they are chosen in a particular form depending on the demands of the composition itself, already formulated, already well and truly in existence. The lines do no more than establish order and clarity on the level of geometrical equilibrium, achieving or claiming to achieve a veritable purification. The regulating lines do not bring in any poetic or lyrical ideas; they do not inspire the theme of the work; they are not creative; they merely establish a balance. A matter of plasticity, pure and simple."

Corbusier was correct. Geometric organization in and of itself does not yield the dynamic concept or inspiration. What it does offer to the creative idea is a process of composition, a means of interrelationship of form, and a method for achieving visual balance. It is a system of bringing the elements together into a cohesive whole.

Although Corbusier writes of the intuitive in geometric organization, my research has shown that in design and architecture it is far less intuitive and far more often a result of knowledge that is thoughtfully applied. Many of the artists, designers, and architects whose work was analyzed in *Geometry of Design* have written about the relationship of geometry to their work. Those that have been involved in education such as Le Corbusier, Josef Müller-Brockmann and Max Bill considered geometric organization and planning essential and fundamental to the design process.

Architecture has some of the strongest educational ties to geometric organization because of the necessity for order and efficiency in construction, and the desire to create aesthetically pleasing structures. The same is not true of art and design. In many schools of art and design the study of geometric organization begins and ends with a discussion of the golden section relationship to the Parthenon in an art history course. This is due in part to the separation of information that is a part of education. Biology, geometry, and art are taught as separate subjects. The content area of each that is congruent to the other is often neglected and the student is left to make the connections on their own. In addition, art and design are commonly viewed as intuitive endeavors and expressions of personal inspiration. Unfortunately, few educators will bring biology or geometry into the studio, or art and design into the science or math classroom. *Geometry of Design* is the result of my efforts to bring some of the congruencies among design, geometry, and biology to my graphic design students.

Kimberly Elam

Acknowledgments

Editorial Services
Christopher R. Elam,
Trumbull, Connecticut

Mathematics Editor
Dr. David Mullins,
Associate Professor of Mathematics,
New College of the University of South
Florida

Special Thanks To:
Mary R. Elam
Charlotte, North Carolina

Johnette Isham
Ringling School of Art and Design

Jeff Maden
Suncoast Porsche, Audi, Volkswagen
Sarasota, Florida

Peter Megert, Visual Syntax Design
Columbus, Ohio

Allen Novak
Ringling School of Art and Design

Jim Skinner
Sarasota, Florida

Jennifer Thompson, Editor
Princeton Architectural Press

Peggy Williams, Conchologist
Sarasota, Florida

Credits:
The analysis of Bruno Monguzzi's
Majakovskij poster is based on an original
analysis by Anna E. Cornett, Ringling
School of Art and Design.

The analysis of Jules Chéret's Folies
Bergère is based on an original analysis
by Tim Lawn, Ringling School of Art and
Design.

Image and Photo Credits

Illinois Institute of Technology Chapel, Photographer – Hedrich Blessing, Courtesy of the Chicago Historical Society

L'Intransigéant, A. M. Cassandre, Collection of Merrill C. Berman

Wagon-Bar, A. M. Cassandre, Collection of Merrill C. Berman

Staatliches Bauhaus Austellung, Fritz Schleifer, Collection of Merrill C. Berman

Der Berufsphotograph, Jan Tschichold, Collection of Merrill C. Berman

Konstruktivisten, Jan Tschichold, Collection of Merrill C. Berman

Pevener, Vantongerloo, Bill, Max Bill, Collection Merrill C. Berman

East Coast by L.N.E.R., Tom Purvis, Collection of the Victoria & Albert Museum

Zeus from Cape Artemision, Photo courtesy of the Greek Ministry of Culture

Furstenberg Porzellan Poster, Inge Druckery

Konkrete Kunst, Max Bill, Courtesy of the Museum für Gestaltung, Zurich

Negerkunst, Max Bill, Courtesy of the Museum für Gestaltung, Zurich

Beethoven, Josef Müller-Brockmann, Photo courtesy of Shizuko Yoshikawa

Musica Viva, 1958, Josef Müller-Brockmann, Photo courtesy of Shizuko Yoshikawa

Musica Viva, 1957, Josef Müller-Brockmann, Photo courtesy of Shizuko Yoshikawa

The Doryphoros (The Spear-Bearer), ca. 440, Roman copy, Jack S. Blanton Museum of Art, The University of Texas at Austin, The William J. Battle collection of Plaster Casts. Photo: Frank Armstrong and Bill Kennedy

Pine Cone Photograph, *Shell* Photographs, *Braun Coffeemaker* Photograph, Allen Novak

Man Inscribed in a Circle, (after 1521), *The Human Figure by Albrecht Dürer, The Complete Dresden Sketchbook*, Dover Publications, Inc., 1972

Façade of the Arsenal of the Piraeus, Notre Dame, 1916 Villa, Towards a New Architecture, Le Corbusier, Dover Publications, 1986

Fechner Tables & Graphs, The Divine Proportion: A Study In Mathematical Beauty, H. E. Huntley, Dover Publications, 1970

Job Poster, Follies Bregère Poster, The Posters of Jules Chéret, Lucy Broido, Dover Publications, Inc., 1992

Human Figure in a Circle, Illustrating Proportions, Leonardo da Vinci, *Leonardo Drawings*, Dover Publications, Inc., 1980

Brno Chair, Ludwig Mies van der Rohe, Courtesy of Knoll

Barcelona Chair, Ludwig Mies van der Rohe, Courtesy of Knoll

Pedestal Chair, Eero Saarinen, Courtesy of Knoll

Chaise Longue, Le Corbusier (Charles Edouard Jeanneret), 1929, Courtesy of Cassina USA

Eames Molded Plywood Chair, Charles Eames & Eero Saarinen, Courtesy Herman Miller, Inc., Photo by Phil Schaafsma

Il Conico Kettle, Aldo Rossi, 1986, Produced by Alessi s.p.a.

Braun Handblender, Photo Courtesy of Braun

Volkswagen New Beetle, Courtesy of Volkswagen of America, Inc.

Selected Bibliography

Alessi Art and Poetry, Fay Sweet, Ivy Press, 1998

A.M. Cassandre, Henri Mouron, Rizzoli International Publications, 1985

Art and Geometry, A Study In Space Intuitions, William M. Ivins, Jr., Dover Publications, Inc., 1964

Basic Visual Concepts and Principles for Artists, Architects, and Designers, Charles Wallschlaeger, Cynthia Busic-Snyder, Wm. C. Brown Publishers, 1992

Contemporary Classics, Furniture of the Masters, Charles D. Gandy A.S.I.D., Susan Zimmermann-Stidham, McGraw-Hill Inc., 1982

The Curves of Life, Theodore Andrea Cook, Dover Publications, Inc., 1979

The Divine Proportion: A Study In Mathematical Beauty, H.E. Huntley, Dover Publications, Inc.,1970

The Elements of Typographic Style, Robert Bringhurst, Hartley & Marks, 1996

50 Years Swiss Poster: 1941-1990, Swiss Poster Advertising Company, 1991

The Form of the Book: Essays on the Morality of Good Design, Jan Tschichold, Hartley & Marks, 1991

The Geometry of Art and Line, Matila Ghyka, Dover Publications, Inc., 1977

The Graphic Artist and His Design Problems, Josef Müller-Brockmann, Arthur Niggli Ltd., 1968

Grid Systems in Graphic Design, Josef Müller-Brockmann, Arthur Niggli Ltd., Publishers, 1981

The Golden Age of the Poster, Hayward and Blanche Cirker, Dover Publications, Inc., 1971

A History of Graphic Design, Philip B. Meggs, John Wiley & Sons, 1998

The Human Figure By Albrecht Dürer, The Complete Dresden Sketchbook, Edited by Walter L. Strauss, Dover Publications, Inc.,1972

Josef Müller-Brockmann, Pioneer of Swiss Graphic Design, Edited by Lars Müller, Verlag Lars Müller, 1995

Leonardo Drawings, Dover Publications, Inc., 1980

Ludwig Mies Van Der Rohe, Arthur Drexler, George Braziller, Inc., 1960

Mathographics, Robert Dixon, Dover Publications, Inc., 1991

Mies Van Der Rohe: A Critical Biography, Franz Schulze, The University of Chicago Press, 1985

The Modern American Poster, J. Stewart Johnson, The Museum of Modern Art, 1983

The Modern Poster, Stuart Wrede, The Museum of Modern Art, 1988

The Modulor 1 & 2, Le Corbusier, Charles Edouard Jeanneret, Harvard University Press, 1954

The Posters of Jules Chéret, Lucy Broido, Dover Publications, Inc., 1980

The Power of Limits: Proportional Harmonies in Nature, Art, and Architecture, Gyorgy Doczi, Shambala Publications, Inc., 1981

Sacred Geometry, Robert Lawlor, Thames and Hudson, 1989

Thonet Bentwood & Other Furniture, The 1904 Illustrated Catalogue, Dover Publications, Inc., 1980

The 20th-Century Poster - Design of the Avant-Garde, Dawn Ades, Abbeville Press, 1984

20th Century Type Remix, Lewis Blackwell. Gingko Press, 1998

Towards A New Architecture, Le Corbusier, Dover Publications, Inc., 1986

Typographic Communications Today, Edward M. Gottschall, The International Typeface Corporation, 1989

Index

A
Alessi, 96
architectural proportions, 20
Art Concrete, 62

B
Barcelona Chair, 56
Barcelona Ottoman, 56
Barcelona Tables, 56
Bauhaus, 52, 72
Bauhaus Ausstellung Poster, 48
Beaux Arts, 58, 70
Beethoven Poster, 78
Begarstaff, 54
Bentwood Rocker, 60
Bill, Max, 5, 62, 72, 75
blue angle fish, 11
Braun, 92, 94
Braun Aromaster Coffee Maker, 94
Braun Handblender, 92
Brno Chair, 60, 61

C
Cassandre, A. M., 50, 64
Chaise Longue, 58
chapel, 76
Chéret, Jules , 44, 46
chromolithography, 46
cognitive preference, 6
comparison, Dürer and da Vinci, 17
Constructivism, 90, 66
Corbusier, 5, 21, 43, 58
Cubism, 51, 52

D
da Vinci, human body proportions, 14
da Vinci, Leonardo , 14, 18
De Stijl, 72
Der Berufsphotograph Poster, 68
Deutsche Industrie Normen, 36
Die Neue Typographie, 66
DIN paper proportioning, 36
Divina Proportione, 14
divine proportion, 20
Doczi, György, 8
Doryphoros
    facial proportions, 18
    body proportions, 12
drawing, human proportions, 14
Druckery, Inge, 88

Dürer, Albrecht, 5, 14, 18
Dürer, body proportions, 14
dynamic rectangles, 32

E
Eames, Charles, 70, 84
East Coast by L.N.E.R. Poster, 54

F
Façade of the Arsenal of the Piraes, 22
facial proportions, 18, 19
Fechner, Gustav, 6
Fibonacci sequence, 10, 29
fish, golden section proportions, 11
Folies-Bergère Poster, 44
Four Books on Human Proportion, 14, 19
Four Constructed Heads, 19
Fürstenberg Porzellan Poster, 88

G
golden ellipse, 30, 98, 99
    Pedestal Chair, 85
    VW Beetle, 99
golden section, 6, 23, 71
    architecture, 20–23
    Brno Chair, 60
    circles and squares, 28
    construction, 24–26
    dynamic rectangles, 32
    ellipse, 30
        East Coast by L.N.E.R. Poster, 54
        Volkswagen Beetle, 99–100
    facial proportions, 18
    Fibonacci Sequence, 29
    fish, 11
    human body, 12, 14, 16, 18
    IIT Chapel, 77
    nature, 8
    Notre Dame Cathedral, 21
    Parthenon, 20
    Pedestal Chair, 84
    pentagon, 30
    Plywood Chair, 70
    preference, 6
    proportional squares, 25
    proportions, 6, 27–28
    rectangle, 6, 24, 98
    shells, 8
    spiral, 25, 31
    square construction, 24

star pentagram, 31, 46, 47
triangle, 30
Folies-Bergère Poster, 44
triangle construction, 26
Greek sculpture, 12
Gropius, Walter, 72
growth patterns, 9

H
harmonic analysis, 20
hexagon construction, 39
hexagonal prism, 38
honeycombs, 38
human body proportions, 14
Human Figure in a Circle, Illustrating Proportions,
14
human proportions, 6

I
Il Conico Kettle, 96
Illinois Institute of Technology Chapel, 76
International Style, 78

J
Jeanneret, Pierre, 58
Job Poster, 46

K
Konkrete Kunst Poster, 72
Konstruktivisten Poster, 66

L
L'Intransigéant Poster, 50
Lalo, 7
Le Corbusier, 5, 21, 43, 101
    Chaise Longue, 58
    regulating lines, 22
Leonardo of Pisa, 29

M
Majakovskij Poster, 90
Man Inscribed in a Circle, 14
Mays, Jay, 98
Mies van der Rohe, 56, 58, 60, 76
Moholy-Nagy, 72
Mouron, Adolphe, 50
MR Chair, 60
Müller-Brockmann, Josef, 5, 78, 81, 82
Musica Viva 1957 Poster, 81
Musica Viva Poster, 82

N
nautilus, 8
Negerkunst Poster, 62
Notre Dame Cathedral, 21

P
Pacioli, Luca, 14
Parthenon, 20
    harmonic analysis, 20
Pedestal Chair, 84
pentagon, 9, 44
pentagram, 9, 45
pentagram page, 67
Pevsner, Vantongerloo, Bill Poster, 75
pine cone, 10
Plywood Chair, 70, 84
Pollio, Marcus Vitruvius, 12
proportion and nature, 8
proportion preferences, 6
proportions, human body, 12
Purvis, Tom, 54

R
rectangle preference, 7
rectangle proportion, 6
regulating lines, 21
root 2 rectangle, 34, 38, 57, 69, 88, 91
    Barcelona Chair, 57
    Beethoven Poster, 78
    construction, circle method, 35
    construction, 34, 73
    Der Berufsphotograph Poster, 68
    diminishing spiral, 35
    dynamic rectangles, 37
    harmonic subdivisions, 37
    Konkrete Kunst Poster, 72
    Majakovskij Poster, 90
    Musica Viva Poster, 82
    Negerkunst Poster, 62
    proportional relationships, 35
    proportions, 63
    Musica Viva, 83
    type construction, 74
root 3 rectangle, 38
root 4 rectangle, 40
root 5 rectangle, 41
root rectangles, comparison, 42
Rossi, Aldo, 96
Russian Constructivists, 90